ISBN 978-0-282-43931-6
PIBN 10851792

English
Français
Deutsche
Italiano
Español
Português

www.forgottenbooks.com

Mythology Photography **Fiction**
Fishing Christianity **Art** Cooking
Essays Buddhism Freemasonry
Medicine **Biology** Music **Ancient**
Egypt Evolution Carpentry Physics
Dance Geology **Mathematics** Fitness
Shakespeare **Folklore** Yoga Marketing
Confidence Immortality Biographies
Poetry **Psychology** Witchcraft
Electronics Chemistry History **Law**
Accounting **Philosophy** Anthropology
Alchemy Drama Quantum Mechanics
Atheism Sexual Health **Ancient History**
Entrepreneurship Languages Sport
Paleontology Needlework Islam
Metaphysics Investment Archaeology
Parenting Statistics Criminology
Motivational

THE LIFE

OF

LIEUTENANT-GENERAL

SIR JOHN MOORE, K.B.

BY HIS BROTHER,

JAMES CARRICK MOORE.

IN TWO VOLUMES.

VOL. I.

LONDON:

JOHN MURRAY, ALBEMARLE-STREET.

MDCCCXXXIII.

LONDON:

Printed by WILLIAM CLOWES,

Stamford-Street.

A STATUE HAVING BEEN ERECTED

TO THE

Memory

OF

JOHN MOORE,

BY THE INHABITANTS OF HIS NATIVE CITY,

THIS HISTORY OF HIS LIFE,

COMPOSED WITH FRATERNAL PIETY,

IS MOST GRATEFULLY

DEDICATED

TO

GLASGOW,

BY THE AUTHOR.

CONTENTS OF VOL. I.

THE LIFE

OF

SIR JOHN MOORE.

CHAPTER I.

BIRTH AND EDUCATION.

SIR JOHN MOORE was born at Glasgow on
the 13th of November, 1761, and, in consequence of the death of two other sons in early
life, became the eldest. Their father, Dr.
Moore, a physician and moral writer, was the
only son of the Reverend Charles Moore, minister of Stirling; whose father was an officer
who served in the wars of King William III.:
and the family by tradition was considered to
be a younger branch of the Moores, or Mures,
of Ruellan, which lineage, however, cannot be
traced. Doctor Moore's mother was the eldest
daughter of John Anderson, Laird of Dovehill,
and of Marian Hay, This lady, entitled, ac-

cording to the usage of that time, the Lady Dovehill, was a reputed descendant of the Earls of Kinnoul. The Andersons of Dovehill are an ancient race, whose estate has been sold, reserving the feudal superiorities, which descended to Sir John Moore, and since to his brother. The doctor married a daughter of Professor Simson of the university of Glasgow, who was niece of Robert Simson the celebrated geometrician.

John Moore, who is now to be considered, was entered at the high school of Glasgow; and Thomas Monro, afterwards so distinguished in India, was one of his schoolfellows. In his boyish days he was fiery and untractable, which faults were gradually suppressed by paternal reproofs, and by his own masculine understanding; so that he acquired a complete command of temper, and a mild disposition. His figure was tall, and graceful, his features were regular, his eyes hazel, hair brown, and the expression of his countenance cheerful and benign. In the year 1772, Dr. Moore was engaged to take charge of Douglas,

Duke of Hamilton, during a tour and residence on the Continent of Europe; and John,
at eleven years of age, was taken with them.
They had hardly reached Paris, when a mis-
chance occurred, which might have had serious
consequences. John, having been left alone,
began, with childish curiosity, to examine the
locks of a pair of loaded pistols. Being ignorant of their mechanism, he accidentally
snapt one of them; the ball pierced through
the wainscot, and wounded a maid-servant in
the adjoining chamber, who screamed aloud.
The doctor, alarmed, ran in, but found his son
safe, and the servant's hurt very slight. John
was deeply affected at having so nearly killed
this poor girl; and his father observed, that
he was thenceforth less heedless.

Not long after this, the Duke of Hamilton,
though five years older, played a similar
prank. It was the custom of the times to
wear swords, and the duke happened to have
on a small hanger. In an idle humour he
drew it, and began to amuse himself by fencing .
at young Moore; and laughed as he forced

him to skip from side to side to shun false thrusts. The duke continued this sport until Moore unluckily started in the line of the sword, and received it in his flank. On feeling himself wounded he exclaimed, 'Ha!' and looked the duke in the face, who, struck with horror, dropt the sword, and rushed out of the room for Dr. Moore. The father on entering saw blood flowing from his son's side: he stript him, and found that the broad blade of the hanger had pierced the skin, and glanced on the outside of the ribs, without penetrating inwardly; the wound was consequently exempt from danger. His agony being relieved, he calmed the terror of the duke. After this event, a warm friendship between the duke and Moore ensued, which only terminated by death. The wound was scarcely closed, when an incident occurred of a less formidable kind. Dr. Moore took his son to walk in the garden of the Tuileries, and while he was looking at some of the statues, John strayed aside to gaze at some French boys whose dress diverted him.

·French children in those days were wont to
be equipped in full formal suits, like little
gentlemen; their hair was powdered, frizzled,
and curled on both sides, and a bag hung
behind: whereas Moore's dress was simple,
according to the custom in England, so the
contrast to each seemed preposterous. The
French boys stared, smiled, and chattered to
each other, while Moore, not understanding a
word of French, could only express his displeasure by gestures. Mutual offence was taken,
and the parties proceeded to hostilities; but
as French boys know nothing of boxing, they
were thrown to the ground one across the
other. Dr. Moore, hearing the outcry, hastened
to the scene: he raised up the discomfited,
and endeavoured to appease their rage. Then
he reprimanded his son for his unmannerly
rudeness, and led him back to the hotel.

Only a short stay was made at Paris, Dr.
Moore being impatient to reach Geneva, a
city better adapted for education, and the ac-
quisition of good morals, than Paris. The

Duke of Hamilton and the doctor were received into the family of a clergyman, eminent for talents and learning; and John was
boarded in a house of education.

, By the.letters of Dr. Moore to his wife at
Glasgow, which have been carefully preserved,
it appears that young Moore, before he was
twelve years of age, had taken an inclination
for the army, which his father did not disap-
prove of, and resolved to have him taught
mathematics and engineering, as soon as he
was fit to learn them. The doctor was well
satisfied with the progress which his son made
in his studies; for, in September 1774, he
wrote to Mrs. Moore, ' You may enjoy all the
' pleasure that a mother ought to feel in the
' certitude of having a most promising son.
' Jack is really a pretty youth; his face is of
' a manly beauty, his person is strong, and
' his figure very elegant. He dances, fences,
' and rides with uncommon address. His
' mind begins to expand, and he shows a great
' deal of vivacity, tempered with good sense

' and benevolence. He is of a daring and
' intrepid temper, and of an obliging disposi-
' tion.

' He draws tolerably; he speaks, reads,
' and writes French admirably well. He has
' a very good notion of geography, arithmetic,
' and the easier parts of practical geometry.
' He is often operating in the fields, and in-
' forms me how he would attack Geneva, and
' shows me the weak part of the fortification.

' The duke and every body are fond of him;
' and he is distractedly fond of his mother
' and sister, and never tires talking of his
' brothers.'

In the above letter no notice is taken of his
knowledge of the Latin language, which was
moderate; but the advantages derived from
his father's superintendency were great. He
prompted him to the study of history, poetry,
and writers of the first class; and by paternal precepts instilled those principles, and
formed that character, which were afterwards
manifested.

A tour into Germany was commenced this

autumn by the Duke of Hamilton, accompanied by Dr. Moore and his son.

At Strasbourg they were entertained by Marshal Contade, the governor, and they afterwards proceeded to Carlsruhe. At this court the Dowager Margravine of Bareith, niece of Prince Ferdinand of Brunswick, took great notice of young Moore. She often questioned him. 'You were at Strasbourg,— did you see Marshal Contade?' 'Yes,' said Jack, 'I had the honour to dine with 'him.' 'And what did you say to him?' He replied, 'I did not say one word to him of 'the battle of Minden, nor of the Prince of 'Brunswick.' The Margravine was delighted with this answer, and often repeated it.

Dr. Moore did not think it advisable to hurry through Germany, but prevailed on the Duke of Hamilton to remain for some time at the principal cities. On these occasions young Moore studied the German language assiduously.

By a passage in a letter from him to me, dated Hanover, May 2, 1775, his passion for the army had increased, for he writes,—' My ' father is constantly with Field - Marshal ' Sporken, who is a fine old soldier, with grey ' hairs, and has been in many battles. He ' loves the English, and is very good to me. ' At Brunswick, the duke got a serjeant, who ' came every day, and taught us the Prussian ' exercise. We are both pretty alert, and ' could fire and charge five times in a minute. ' We fired thirty times each the last day of ' our exercise.'

Towards the end of the month they reached Berlin, and were received with distinction by Frederic II. The Prussian army, organised by that great tactician, was considered the best disciplined in Europe. The Duke of Hamilton and his friends readily obtained permission to be present at the reviews. These continued for three days on a grand scale; for nearly forty thousand infantry, cavalry, and artillery, were manœuvred in imitation of a real action. The splendour of the spectacle, accompanied with martial music, and the

thunder of the guns, fascinated young Moore ;
and his father wrote,—' If Jack had hesitated
' about being a soldier, this glorious scene
' would have confirmed him.'

. Among the King of Prussia's generals, there
was none in higher estimation than the old
Earl Marischal of Scotland, who is so finely
eulogised by Rousseau. As he retained a
warm attachment to his native country, he
was delighted with the arrival of the premier
Scottish peer ; and he had many conferences
with Dr. Moore, who in his youth had seen
the Highland army under Prince Charles
Stuart, at the siege of Stirling. The re-
membrance of that memorable expedition,
with its disastrous consequences, greatly affected the earl ; yet he frequently renewed
the subject, having had so deep a share in the
fallen fortunes of the House of Stuart. He
took a considerable liking to young Moore ;
and finding that the love of arms was riveted
in his mind, he presented him with a pair of
Prussian pistols, and also a small pocket -

Horace, which classic became his favourite.
These valuable testimonials continue to be
carefully preserved by me.

In the month of August, the travellers
reached Vienna, and obtained introductions
to the Imperial Court. At that time the most
brilliant expectations were entertained of
Joseph II., which vanished before the termination of his brief reign. He was singularly
curious respecting foreigners, and sometimes
deigned to converse familiarly with Dr.
Moore, who made so favourable an impression on the emperor's mind, that he offered
to take his son into his service, and gave
assurances of his advancement. This proposal, however flattering, was declined: indeed, Moore had too much love for his native
country, to consent to live and serve in another. His natural bias appears in the following passage of a letter to his brother
Graham, at Glasgow:—

‘ I am pleased, my dear boy, that you wish
‘ to be a sailor, for I am sure you will be a
‘ brave one. I hope that, in some years after

' this, you and I will thresh the Monsieurs,
' both by sea and land ; but I hope we won't
' make war with the Spaniards ; for the
' Spanish ambassador is the best and kindest
' man I ever saw.

'Vienna, Oct. 21, 1775.'

Italy was lastly visited. Their stay at
Venice, at that time a city of great dissipation, was short. Towards the end of November, the party reached Rome, and Dr. Moore
was filled with those vivid emotions, which
the recollection of its former greatness is
calculated to excite. In a letter to Mrs.
Moore, he writes :—

' I have not yet time to give you my sen-
' timents on the wonders I have seen ; only,
' I must assure you that the Roman history
' never gave me such a high idea of that
' amazing people, as the remains of their
' grandeur, which are still to be found here.
' The first day I ran to the Capitol, to Tra-
' jan's Pillar, to the Pantheon, and to St.
Peter's, that I might satiate myself with a

' general view before I could wait for mi-
' nutiæ.'

The son was too young to be equally
affected as his father with the sight of
Rome, once the centre whence radiated to
the world, arts, knowledge, and civilization. The acquisitions derived from travelling on the Continent of Europe by different individuals are various. Some return
sprinkled with affectations, or stained with
vices: while others bring back polished
manners, elegant tastes, and enlarged under-
standings; and, perhaps, the greater number
acquire such a portion of each, as to render
it doubtful to which side the balance inclines.
In order to seize the good, and eschew the
evil, on such occasions, paternal watchfulness
is peculiarly useful.

Naples, one of the most delightfully situated cities in the world, was next visited.
In a letter from the doctor to Mrs. Moore,
he states,—

' As Jack expressed a great desire to
' attend me to Naples, I took him with me,

' and he visited with attention and relish the
' many curiosities of the place. We ascended
' Vesuvius together, when that mountain was
' in a very angry mood, and his eagerness
' led him a little too near the mouth of the
' crater, when it happened to vomit up a
' great quantity of lava, and burning stones.
' A gentleman in company called to Jack to
' run, and showed him the example. As they
' were running away upon the glowing cinders,
' Jack fell, and wounded his knee and thigh
' so much as to be laid up for some days. But
' he was well quit, for the lava and stones fell
' in such a quantity, on the place from which
' they had run with so much precipitation,
' that, in all likelihood, they would have been
' destroyed had they remained. Jack, on
' the whole, was in as much danger, and as
' well wounded, as if he had stood a tolerable
' brisk siege.'

When at Naples the glad tidings arrived
that the Duke of Argyle had obtained an
ensigncy in the 51st regiment for young
John. His joy was boundless, but as he was

only fifteen years of age, leave of absence from the regiment then at Minorca was obtained, and he continued some months longer with his father, and acquired the Italian language. The party repassed the Alps in midsummer, and after some stay at Geneva reached Paris. There the ensign quitted his father, to fly to Glasgow.

I still recollect his mother's transports on embracing her eldest son, who had left her when a wild schoolboy, and had returned an accomplished youth. Absence had stamped filial and fraternal love deeper in his heart. We, his brethren, looked with surprise at the alteration years had produced; and wondered that our brother should already wear a sword.

What happiness did he then bring to his mother! What a reverse when she lost him!

Chapter II.

MOORE'S ENTRANCE INTO THE ARMY.—MINORCA.
—PENOBSCOT.

BEFORE two short months had flown past,
Ensign Moore quitted his mother and family
at Glasgow, and hastened to Marseilles, where
he embarked for Minorca, which he reached
early in the year 1777.

In the fortress of Port Mahon, commanded
by the veteran General Murray, he was taught
the rudiments of military discipline; the drill,
the manual exercise, regimental duties, the
nightly watches, and all the military forms to
prevent surprises, and secure the garrison.
Murray was a man of high character, and a
strict disciplinarian, but of a violent temper.
Moore, however, acquired his good opinion by
the exact performance of his duty. He was
superior to the fopperies of many young officers, who deviate in dress as much as they

dare, from the precise uniform : and love to display a false spirit by disobeying orders whenever they believe they will escape detection.   In letters to his father, he commended highly his regiment and the officers. He was pleased with the island, and expressed surprise that some officers should think it dull; which irksome feeling, his cheerful temper, and the studies prosecuted by his father's admonitions, entirely prevented.   In a letter to his mother, he observes, ' I am very ' intimate with two or three of the officers, ' and I am upon a bad footing with none of ' them. I never have had the misfortune to ' have a quarrel with anybody since I ' joined the regiment; so never was I happier ' in my life, save those seven weeks I passed ' with you, dear mother! in Glasgow.'

As there was no appearance that Minorca would be attacked, and as the American war was then raging, Moore cast a wistful eye to that scene, and wrote his wishes to his father. These were gratified in a manner he scarcely expected; for his friend the Duke of Hamilton

became fired with a transitory passion for the
army, and sent in proposals to government to
raise a regiment for immediate service.   Lord
North, the prime minister, accepted the offer;
the regiment was raised, and the Duke obtained the commission of captain; he also
seized this opportunity of getting promotion
for his young friend, who was immediately
sent for, and advanced to the rank of lieutenant, and was also appointed paymaster.   By
this double appointment, which was then
usual, a knowledge of regimental accounts,
and of other military details, was attained.

The command of the Hamilton regiment
was given to Brigadier-general MacLean,
who for some years had held high rank in the
Portuguese service.   He was an officer of rare
merit.   As soon as six companies were raised
and trained, they were embarked for Halifax
in Nova Scotia, but the Duke of Hamilton
did not accompany them.   The passion of
glory was superseded by that of love; his
Grace married, and resigned his commission.

These young troops, among whom was

Lieutenant Moore, reached their destination in safety, where they continued in garrison, until more actively employed. Sir Henry Clinton, Commander-in-chief of the British army, thought it advisable to take possession of the Bay of Penobscot, and to build a fort, as a maritime station, to interrupt the trade of Boston. Brigadier MacLean was ordered to perform this service, who embarked with a few troops, among which were the six companies of the Hamilton regiment. In June, 1779, this detachment sailed with a favourable wind, and proceeded to the river Penobscot. The troops were landed on a woody and deserted coast, and the General, after examining the country, selected the proper spot upon which to erect a fort. The officer of engineers was ordered to draw out a plan; but the General detected numerous imperfections in his designs. It was not without difficulty, and after many alterations, that a tolerable one was procured. Then the felling of trees, and the construction of the fort commenced with alacrity. This operation excited a very

serious alarm among the citizens of Boston,
ever jealous of their commerce ; who, having
intelligence that the British were few in num i
ber, resolved to overwhelm them with a superior force.   The exertions made on this
occasion by that city were extraordinary : for
in a few weeks six large frigates, thirteen
stout privateers, and twenty-four transports
were equipped and filled with 3000 troops,
and stores of every species requisite for a
siege.

On the 25th of July, this fleet was descried
steering to the mouth of the river Penobscot,
when the walls of the fort were not yet breast
high.

The General, experienced in resources, instantly reduced the plan of the works, and
hastened their construction, to render them
in some degree defensible.

During this bustle ashore, the American
fleet sailed up the river, and anchored nearly
opposite to the unfinished fort ; but the inter-
vening woods concealed the operations of the
British. Next day, after a cautious examina-

tion of the coast, some troops were put into boats to make a descent. But, on approaching the shore, they were fired at by a party concealed behind trees, which arrested the Americans, who rowed back to their shipping. Similar ineffectual attempts to land were made on the two subsequent days. At length the Americans, instructed by these miscarriages, made preparations to overcome all opposition, and to disembark their whole force. Early in the morning, three ships of war, arranged with their broadsides towards the shore, opened a heavy fire of round and double-headed shot upon the wood. The roaring of the guns, the falling of the trees, and the crashing of their branches, astounded the young soldiers: when suddenly the cannonading ceased, and boats full of troops were rowed off to the beach. It happened on that day, that a company of the Hamilton regiment formed the picket to oppose the landing, and Lieutenant Moore was posted on the left with only twenty men under his orders. The captain who commanded, unused to action, ordered the soldiers not to fire until the enemy landed ; so the Americans undisturbed rowed briskly till their boats grounded, then, giving a shout, they sprang on shore. The British, who were only recruits, saw the great superiority of the numbers of the enemy ; they fired a volley, and ran back in disorder. Lieutenant Moore called to his small party, ' Will the Hamilton men leave me? Come ' back, and behave like soldiers.' They obeyed, and recommenced firing. The Americans returned the fire, without venturing to advance into the wood. Moore observed their commanding officer flourishing his sword, and encouraging his men. He levelled his piece, for subalterns then carried fusils, and he believed that he could have killed him ; but he replaced his firelock on his shoulder without discharging it. While this resistance was persevered in on the left, the rest of the detachment reached the fort, and the captain reported to the general, that the enemy had landed in great numbers, and forced the picket to retreat. ' But where is Moore?'

said General MacLean; 'He is, I fear, cut
: off.' 'What then is the firing I still hear?'
'He could not tell.' The General then commanded Captain Dunlop with his company
to march to the shore, and repel the enemy,
or bring off Lieutenant Moore. Moore was
found by Captain Dunlop at his post, still
holding the Americans at bay. But as they
were advancing on both flanks, Dunlop saw
that it was necessary to retire to prevent
being surrounded. He therefore ordered
Moore to form in the rear of the column the
remains of his party, for seven out of the
twenty had fallen ; and the detachment
marched back to the fort in good order. In
a letter to his father, Moore wrote, 'I was
'upon picket the morning the rebels landed.
'I got some little credit, by chance, for
'my behaviour during the engagement.
'To tell you the truth, not for anything
'that deserved it, but because I was the
'only officer who did not leave his post
'*too soon.* I confess that at the first fire they
'gave us, which was within thirty yards, I

'was a good deal startled, but I think this 'went gradually off afterwards.' On the return of the detachment, the general learned from Moore the particulars that had occurred, and he expected that the Americans flushed with success would immediately storm the unfinished works, when the garrison were in consternation by the cannonade, and the repulse of the pickets. Measures for defence were immediately adopted : the works were lined with troops and instructions given to the officers on every event. The General gave Moore the command of fifty men, posted in reserve, with orders, 'that 'should the enemy rush forward, as soon as 'they got into the ditch of the fort, he should 'sally out and attack them on the flank with 'charged bayonets.' But the Americans were not so enterprising, for being somewhat disconcerted by the loss which they had sustained, they took up a position out of the reach of the guns of the fort, and remained tranquil.

For some days they were busied in landing

artillery and stores, for a regular siege, and
only skirmishing occurred. At length they
broke ground, and raised a battery at about
twelve hundred yards from the fort: this
opened early in the morning, and the new
levies, of which the garrison was composed,
were much alarmed. The General, hearing
this, came forth from his tent, and observing
that the officers and men, none of whom had
ever seen service before, were stooping their
heads at every shot, he reproached them
sharply; and calling for his aide-de-camps
went to the gate, and commanded it to be
thrown open. Then walking erect towards
the battery, he examined it with his spy-
glass: ' You see,' he said, ' there is no dan-
' ger from the fire of these wretched artillery-
' men.' After this observation, he returned
deliberately, and ordered the gate to be
closed. This behaviour of their General inspired the garrison with so much courage,
that there was no risk afterwards of their
shrinking from their duty.

The approaches of the Bostonians were

much retarded by the skill of General
MacLean : yet a train of heavy artillery, and
superior numbers, might at last have prevailed. But after a siege of three weeks,
Commodore Sir George Collier, apprized of
the danger, arrived off Penobscot bay, with a
line-of-battle ship, and a few frigates. Before
this squadron could be seen from the fort, it
was discovered from the topmasts of the American ships ; and in the course of the night
the besieging army hastily reimbarked. Next
morning the American fleet drew up in line,
making a show of resistance : on the approach
of the British, however, this resolution was
relinquished, and an attempt was made to
escape up the river. But their ships of war,
intermingled with the transports, were closely
chased and driven on shore. Some were captured, others set fire to by their own crews,
who leaped out and fled into the woods.
Yet these disasters did not soon terminate ;
for the seamen and soldiers accused each
other of cowardice. They fought : many
lives were thus lost, others perished by

famine, and the remainder reached Boston in a miserable plight. General MacLean having finished the construction of the fort, left in it a sufficient garrison, and returned to Halifax with the Hamilton regiment. Moore's sentiments on commencing the rudiments of war are thus expressed in a letter to his father:—

'You may conceive, dear Father; how 'happy this siege has made us, independent 'of the success we met with; as to see a 'little service was what all along we had 'been wishing for. Your friend, Dunlop,* 'who happened to command the regiment 'during the siege, got very deservedly credit 'for his activity: he exerted himself more 'than anybody there.'

In this first essay of arms, Moore acquired the warm friendship of General Francis MacLean, from whom he was wont to say he had derived much instruction. This experienced officer had a library of the best military books in the French and German

---

* This excellent officer died a brigadier in the West Indies.

languages, and had studied his profession thoroughly. But merit is often lost from being unknown. In this instance it was recognised too late, for he was about to be employed in a conspicuous station, when his health failed. Previously he had resided long in Portugal, which had rendered his constitution unable to sustain the frigid climate of Nova Scotia. He perished that winter deeply lamented, and never forgotten by his young friend.

After this, Halifax being remote from active warfare, became a spiritless quarter to Moore. He, however, was promoted to the rank of captain, and then applied for leave to go to New York, the head-quarters of the commander-in-chief.

Our brother Graham was about this period engaged for the first time in action, being a midshipman in Lord Byron's fleet, when he fought the Count D'Estaign, near Grenada; and it happened that I had gone to America, as a medical officer, a safer employment. On returning from Virginia, I

landed late at night at New York, in a very
melancholy mood, as I did not imagine that
there was a single individual in that city who
knew me.   I went to a coffee-house to seek a
bed for the night, where, to my astonishment,
I found my beloved brother John.

‘ O, qui complexus et gaudia quanta fuerunt !’

My vexations were now reversed.   We lived
together, first at New York, and after a few
weeks at a Dutch farmer's house on Long
Island, while eventful public occurrences were
proceeding.   For Lord Cornwallis's army,
which I had just left, was invested by the combined forces of France and America : every
attempt to relieve him was frustrated ; and the
capitulation at York Town, in Virginia, put
an end to the American contest.

That winter a large fleet being about to sail
for England, my brother and I procured passages in a transport with invalid soldiers.   We
had scarcely sailed through Sandy Hook, when
a hurricane arose and dispersed the fleet ;
some ships were blown to the West Indies, and
a few were taken by the enemy, or lost at sea.

Our transport was a stout vessel, with a good crew which stood the tempest well. At the mouth of the British channel we were chased, early in the morning, by a privateer; which being ascertained by our glasses, the officers, among whom was my brother, prepared the ship for action. The British flag was displayed, the guns were loaded, and those invalids who were able to fight were arrayed with their firelocks on the deck. In the mean time, the privateer, without shewing colours, came dashing on under a cloud of canvass, and got into our wake. The crew were all kept concealed, the captain only appearing. I watched him from the poop, expecting every instant a broadside to be fired off. Instead of which, seeing our soldiers and preparations, he hailed us with his trumpet, put a few frivolous questions, and then dropping astern, sheered off. The military men might be vexed, but I was contented with this bloodless conclusion of the chase, contemning the glory of beating off a paltry privateer.

Next day we anchored in Falmouth harbour, and my brother and I posted to London. Our father was then busily engaged in writing Zeluco, and our mother, who knew we were on the seas, was listening day and night to every gust of wind that blew. When she saw us both rush into the house, she could hardly trust to her dazzled sight. Except Graham, who was cruising on the Western Ocean, the family were all again assembled. The re-union of the dispersed members of an affectionate family creates heartfelt emotions never experienced by insulated individuals.

Chapter III.

PEACE.—MOORE IN PARLIAMENT.—PROMOTED TO
THE RANK OF A FIELD OFFICER.—ORDERED TO
IRELAND, AND AFTERWARDS TO GIBRALTAR.

In the year 1783 peace was proclaimed with
France, Spain, Holland, and the United States
of America. This event, beneficial to the
nation, was regretted by those merchants,
contractors, and artificers who were engaged
in furnishing warlike stores, and by naval and
military officers panting for promotion. The
Hamilton regiment being disbanded, Captain
Moore was reduced upon half-pay. This was
a critical period; for idleness is often the
cause of hapless propensities which debase
the mind, and of slothful habits which hinder
future exertions. But Moore lived with his
family, and his time was not mispent. He
resumed the studies of field-fortification and
tactics; and he augmented his general know-

ledge by reading the works of good authors. He was also introduced into society by his father, and his own manners were so prepossessing, that he easily extended his acquaintance, for his disposition tended to form friendships. In conversation he was neither voluble nor obtrusive, but unassuming and sensible; with his intimates open and cheerful, but in large companies rather reserved. He usually spent a couple of months in autumn with the Duke of Hamilton, in Scotland, and visited there his relatives and early friends, whom in his highest prosperity he never neglected.

The bad success of the American war occasioned the downfal of the ministry; and a violent contest occurred for the settlement of a new administration. After several changes, William Pitt obtained the ascendency; to overwhelm whom, Lord North and Charles Fox formed the notorious coalition, a political fault which blighted the fame of both: for both having long professed opposite political principles, their union proved that these had either been assumed, or were now abandoned. But over-confidence in their rhetorical powers persuaded them that they could excuse to the nation this gross inconsistency; and, relying on a majority in parliament thus acquired, they attempted to seize the patronage of India, and almost to wrench the sceptre from the King's hands. In this emergency the genius of Pitt shone forth: whose eloquence roused the indignation of the country against this political junto, who were dismissed from their offices, and the parliament which sanctioned the coalition was dissolved.

In the new parliament, Captain Moore was elected a representative of four Scottish boroughs, through the influence of the Duke of Hamilton, but was left freely to follow his own judgment on every measure. Indeed, unless unfettered, he would have declined the seat: for, though his circumstances were narrow, the qualities of his mind rendered him independent. By regular attendance in the House, and by listening to

the orations of the most eloquent men which
this country has yet produced, he improved his
knowledge of the fabric and spirit of the constitution, and gained an insight into the conduct of statesmen. Being convinced that
Mr. Pitt was animated with the love of his
country, and that his measures were directed
towards its welfare, he generally voted for
them; and his political conduct was such,
that Mr. Burke, though then of the opposite
party, commended him highly to his father,
with whom he was intimate.

It is obviously the interest of every minister, that the nation should prosper; but of
his opponents, unfortunately, that it should
not; which accounts for the usual conduct of
the two parties, and of their frequent inconsistency when in and out of office. This,
which is in the nature of things, has been
often complained of: it explains why, even
bad men have sometimes proved good ministers; and why honourable men, when
leaders in opposition, and contending for
wealth and power, have become so irri-

tated by disappointment, and transported
by ambition, as to be tempted to rouse
up popular discontents and tumults, reckless of their consequences. The subver-
sion of the ancient democracies proceeded
from this cause; but the British constitution
had been preserved from a similar fate, by a
happy mixture of monarchy and aristocracy.
Should these be subverted and democracy
predominate, experience evinces that anarchy
and despotism will follow. The moderation
of Moore's character prevented his becoming
a violent party-man. He was acquainted
with persons of opposite political opinions,
and being in the heyday of youth lived gaily
and in good company. He even had the
felicity of becoming acquainted with the
Duke of York, a prince ever constant to his
friends.

But neither civil contentions, nor all the
pleasures of the capital altered or diminished
his ruling passion; he continued anxiously
desirous of military rank. No opportunity
however occurred until the year 1787, when

two new battalions were added to the 60th
regiment, to one of which he was appointed
Major. Then escaping from London and all
its allurements, he flew to Chatham where
the recruits were assembling. His spirits,
which from lack of employment had become
languid, were now stirred up by the drum and
fife; and the drill became his morning business. The complete command he possessed
over his own temper qualified him peculiarly
for disciplining troops. Towards the officers
under his command his conduct was friendly,
yet firm; towards the soldiers kind, but
strict; and to both impartially just. The
battalion which he formed after a few
months was reviewed, and its appearance
and discipline were extolled by the reviewing
General. Next year Moore was appointed
Major to the 51st regiment, that in which he
had got his first commission. It was quartered at Cork, to which city he soon repaired.
The regiment at that time was a very indif-
ferent one, but every attempt or suggestion
he threw out for its improvement was

thwarted or disapproved of by the Lieutenant-
Colonel, from jealousy of interference. On
perceiving this, he neither spoke nor entered
into any cabal against his commanding
officer; but relinquished all hope of amelio-
rating the state of the regiment. He performed his own duty precisely, and by living
in the mess on familiar terms with the officers,
he had the opportunity of discovering their
respective talents and defects. Ensign Anderson, who afterwards became his insepa-
rable companion, was among them. There
were several others with whom he formed
friendships, and whose advancement he subsequently promoted.

Ireland was in a state of tolerable tranquillity and contentment, as the caballers of
that period had not decided on rebellion.
The frank hospitality and diverting humours
of the Irish gentlemen, and the beauty and
lively manners of the ladies, were exceedingly
agreeable to Major Moore. Jollity and re-
velry abounded, in which he joined freely,
not being much impeded by regimental

affairs; for, to avoid giving offence, he took little share in them.

In the midst of this dissipation a rumour suddenly arose of a war with Spain, in consequence of a trifling mercantile dispute, on the bleak coast of Nootka Sound. Our minister was then young and sanguine; and being emulous of his father's fame, was more desirous of restoring the glory of Great Britain, somewhat faded in the last unhappy war, than of shunning contests with foreign powers. He raised an armament; projected an expedition against South America, and demanded from Spain satisfaction for an aggression asserted to have been committed on some British merchants at Nootka. On this occasion orders were issued to the 51st regiment, among others, to prepare for foreign service. This annunciation was received joyfully by all except the Lieutenant-Colonel, who being a family man, perceived that a campaign in Cuba or the Caraccas might be incommodious. He, therefore, applied at the War-office for leave to retire. This was

acceded .to, and Moore purchased. his commission, thus acquiring the rank of Lieûte-
nant-Colonel.

. . The command of. the. regiment, which. was
in a very disordered state, now devolved upon.
Moore,. whose character improved by advancement.   He immediately commenced
rectifying the discipline; but in the execution difficulties were necessarily encountered :
for the British youth, being less accustomed
to restraint than those of other countries,
yield more reluctantly to subordination,
which is indispensable in an army. To overcome this repugnance, without exciting animosity, requires considerable address. Some
commanding officers, by too great familiarity
with those subordinate to them, lose their
authority; others by arrrogance stir up
hatred and opposition. It requires propriety,
combined with dignity of manners, to enable
a commander to live on amicable terms with
his officers, and enforce strict military regulations. Moore, who was bent on forming the.
regiment for every military .duty, inspired his .

officers with the same desire ; and gradually rendered the soldiers dexterous in the use of arms, and rapid in their evolutions. In all points of discipline which are useful on service he was rigid : but in other matters, being desirous of gratifying the soldiers, and of increasing their comforts, he was indulgent, and even disposed to overlook slight neglects. At that time the practice of excessive drinking was prevalent in the army, and even among the officers. This he resolved to abolish in the regiment without delay. He signified in very strong terms his determination on this subject to his officers, who expressed their approbation and assured him of their concurrence. Yet one untractable Lieutenant, in spite of warnings, appeared on the parade staggering from intoxication. He was compelled immediately to quit the service, and no more examples of that kind were requisite. There were, however, a few others accustomed to relaxed discipline, who did not relish the change of system. These successively exchanged into other corps, and were replaced by young gentlemen of superior energy.

The character which the 51st regiment attained, and the spirit it afterwards displayed in a long war, on a variety of perilous occasions, were proofs of excellent training.

Spain being in no condition to cope in war with Great Britain, gave the satisfaction that was demanded, which put an end to the preparation for invading South America.

The 51st regiment remained in Ireland until 1792, when it was ordered to embark for Gibraltar. In a letter to his father he gives the following particulars :—

'Brunswick Transport, Cove of Cork, 8th March, 1792.

'My dear Father,

      . . . . 'I have been hurried
' to death with the embarkation; the new
' serjeant-major I had been obliged to ap-
' point, not being conversant with the busi-
' ness. But I have been much pleased with
' the behaviour of the regiment. Their or-
' derly conduct upon leaving a town like

' Cork, in which they had formed many ac-
' quaintances, was more than I could have
' expected. Upon the parade, the evening
' before we marched, I told them they might
' enjoy themselves, and be jolly with their
' friends till nine, when I expected every
' man to be in his quarters; and that at
' seven next morning they should come sober
' to the parade ready to march. They were
' glorious that night : however, with a very
' few exceptions, they retired to their quar-
' ters at nine, and came next morning (to
' the parade) perfectly sober. We lost one
' man only by desertion since we received
' orders to embark, and we recovered him
' yesterday. . . . . It rained during the
' march (to the Cove), and the roads were
' very deep ; but whilst the commissary was
' mustering us on the beach, it cleared, and
' turned out a very fine afternoon.

' Two other regiments were arranged upon
' the beach waiting for the return of the boats,
' the sun was shining and the sea perfectly
' calm. I ordered none of the boats to put off

' till the whole regiment was embarked, that
' all might proceed together.   By signal we
' gave three cheers, which were answered by
' the regiments on shore : the bands playing,
' colours flying, &c., the whole forming a
' lively, animating scene.   In ten minutes we
' were rowed aboard our different ships. . .
' and at day-light to-morrow, if the wind con-
' tinues fair, we sail.'

Chapter IV.

ARRIVAL AT GIBRALTAR—SAILS TO CORSICA —OPERATIONS IN THAT ISLAND.

To attain eminence in any profession, the mind must be intensely fixed upon its principles, and the individual experienced in its practice. For military improvement, Gibraltar is a less favourable school than a camp, yet it presents some advantages. For the garrison is numerous and is daily drilled, manœuvred and employed on various duties: while the bomb-proof casemates, the ramparts, and the cannon pointed towards the sea and shore, together with the Spanish lines across the peninsula, fill the imagination with martial ideas. Moreover, the memorable defence which this fortress maintained for seven years, against the fleets and armies of France and Spain, aided by formid-

able floating batteries; which last were destroyed by red-hot balls, with a piteous loss of
lives, has converted this Herculean pillar into
a stupendous monument of British prowess.
That terrible catastrophe was so fresh in re-
membrance, that Buonaparte never assailed
this citadel, which is deemed impregnable.
Moore, on his arrival, wrote as follows:

'Gibraltar, 26th March, 1792.

'My dear Father,

   'I have only time to tell you that, after a
'most delightful passage, we anchored in this
'Bay, the eleventh day from our leaving Cork.
'We only landed yesterday, and every thing
'is so completely opposite to the arrange-
'ments in Britain or Ireland, that we are
'much at a loss, and must continue so for
'some time, in spite of every exertion on my
'part. I have been up at daylight ever since
'we anchored, and seldom off my legs till
'bedtime. The weather is that of a hot July
'in England. Oranges, green peas, &c. are
'in perfection; and notwithstanding the de-

' scriptions I had of the rock, it surprised me
' more than any place I ever saw. Sir Robert
' Boyd (the Lieutenant-Governor) acknow-
' ledged me as an old acquaintance, and has
' been extremely civil.' . . . .

But after the novelty of the views from this
extraordinary place was over, and when his
regiment was brought to perfect discipline,
the monotony of garrison duty began to be
felt. Colonel Moore had already travelled
over a portion of America, and a great part of
Europe ; but travelling does not soon produce
satiety, and the neighbouring cities of Spain
were tempting objects. He accordingly obtained permission, and visited Cadiz, Xeres,
and Seville. This excursion gave him great
amusement, after which it appeared that he
returned to his duty with fresh ardour. But
he was not fated to repeat jaunts of pleasure ;
for in this very year there arose, consequent
to a revolution in France, a war the most
memorable that ever happened, from the im-
mensity of the treasures expended, from the
vast space to which the warfare reached, and

from the multitude of forces by sea and land which were engaged and destroyed during its continuance. Not only Europe, but a great portion of Asia, Africa, and America were convulsed by this contention : and the vicissitudes of fortune were so remarkable, that France at one period gained by many victories such augmented dominion and pre-eminent power, as to force into a league against Great Britain, North America and almost the whole of the European States. But the latter, at length, bursting their chains, poured forth their forces against their vanquisher, who, was repulsed and discomfited; and France, being in her turn invaded, and the capital taken, was compelled to yield to the terms dictated by her enemies.

Soon after the commencement of these transactions, a body of French loyalists occupied Toulon, and invited a British and Spanish force into that city. These were presently besieged by a numerous army of French republicans; and in December, 1793, the 50th and 51st regiments were embarked

at Gibraltar to reinforce the garrison of
Toulon: but before they could reach their
destination, the besieged were repulsed in an
unsuccessful sally, and General O'Hara, the
commander, was wounded and captured; on
which the garrison, being too weak to maintain the works against a much superior army,
embarked on board their ships. The greater
part of the French men-of-war were then
burned in the harbour, and the unhappy royalists, to escape from the fury of the republicans, took refuge in the British fleet, which
sailed to Hieres Bay.

Intelligence of these disastrous events were
received by the convoy with the troops from
Gibraltar, which therefore proceeded to the
same place : but a frigate, which had on board
the baggage of the 51st regiment, separated
from the fleet in the night, and the captain,
deceived by the English colours hoisted on
the ramparts of Toulon, sailed into the harbour and was taken. This was a severe loss
to both officers and men; for Moore had ordered every thing to be procured and put on

board that could contribute to their conveni-
ency, and be useful on service. It was late in
the evening of the last day of December, that
the transports entered Hieres Bay, when immediately Moore went on board the Victory,
Lord Hood's flag-ship. He presented a statement of his regiment, together with the orders
which he had received from Sir Robert Boyd,
to his Lordship, who expressed some surprise
at the smallness of the number of men, and
said, ' You have come rather late.' He then
turned to a navy officer with whom he had been
transacting business. Moore, after this dry
reception, retired into the outer cabin to join
General Dundas, the commander of the army.
Every part of the Admiral's ship was crowded
with French men and women of the principal
families of Toulon, who had made their escape
the night the town was evacuated. Moore
hearing the sound of a violin and of dancing
in the ward-room, made some enquiry, and
was much surprised to learn that the French
were dancing out the old year merrily. Yet
few of them had anything but the clothes on

their backs, and the prospect before them was most gloomy. They contrived, however, to forget the past, to suppress all thoughts of the future, and, for the present, to make themselves happy.

Consultations took place between the Admiral and the General respecting future operations, and Corsica became the principal subject of their deliberations. This island had revolted from France, and the aged and patriotic chief, Paoli, placed at the head of their affairs, had applied for succours to England. It was at length resolved, that Colonel Moore and Major Koehler, an excellent artillery officer, should be sent to Corsica, to examine how far an attack upon that island, with the small military force embarked, was advisable. Sir Gilbert Elliot, the King's commissioner in the Mediterranean, was to accompany them, to communicate with Paoli on political points.

This deputation accordingly sailed (*Jan. 14th*) in a frigate, and landed in the little Isle of Rossa, whence they proceeded to Murato. The inhabitants of every village through which they passed saluted them with vollies of musketry, and exclaimed ' Viva Paoli, la patria, è la nazione Inglese!' This reception was very amusing; and they found that Paoli had taken up his residence at a convent of Recollets, which had been abandoned since the revolution. The convent was surrounded with armed peasants, who came voluntarily from different parts of the island, and served without pay. They carried on their backs ten days provisions, consisting chiefly of dried chestnuts; and returned home, when their food was consumed. But others succeeded, from the strong attachment felt by all the natives to Paoli, who had commanded their armies in former wars against the Genoese and French. After the first compliments, the subject of the mission began to be discussed; when General Paoli addressed himself to the two military gentlemen, to explain to them the operations which he wished to be adopted. But Colonel Moore informed him, that Sir Gilbert

Elliot. was the King's Commissioner, with
whom in the first place the business must be
agreed upon. To this Paoli made some odd
answer, that he was tired. with ministers
and negotiations. He then, however, turned
to Sir Gilbert, and said, ' I wrote long ago to
' the King and to his ministers, that I and
' my people wished to be free either as sub-
' jects, or under the protection of Great Bri-
' tain, as the King and the country may
' think most convenient. I wish before I
' die, to see my country, after various strug-
' gles, during these three hundred years,
' settled and happy, with a proper degree of
' liberty, under the protection or government
' of the British nation.' The General was so
much affected whilst he spoke, that tears
gushed into his eyes. The conference was
conducted amicably, Sir Gilbert giving assurances of assistance for the expulsion of
the French. Next morning, Moore and
Major Koehler rode out to reconnoitre St.
Fiorenza and the neighbouring country.
The Signor Pozzo di Borgo accompanied

them, and an escort of above forty volun-
teers. They fell in with a French party and
a slight skirmish ensued, in which the Corsicans acted well. When the French were
driven off, St. Fiorenza, the works of Martello, and the fort of Fornelli were accurately
examined, and Major Koehler made sketches
of the ground.

After their return, the landing of the troops
and the military operations were canvassed
with General Paoli, and Moore was struck
with the intelligence he displayed; indeed,
he reminded him of his old friend General
Francis MacLean. Paoli was then very aged,
and much afflicted at the recent loss of his
brother; a man so much beloved and vene-
rated by the Corsicans, that they believed
him a saint, and were convinced that by his
intercession in heaven they would gain their
independence. The principal business being
agreed upon, Sir Gilbert sailed to the Isle of
Elba, to make arrangements respecting the
French royalists, who had been landed there.
Moore remained for some days to examine

the coast, and particularly the town of Calvi.
After which Lord Hood's fleet appearing, he
went off in a boat at night, though it blew
hard, and got on board the Victory. Major
Koehler was left with Paoli. Moore then
presented to Lord Hood and General Dundas a full statement of the intelligence he
had obtained, and the observations he had
made on the state of the French fortresses,
together with drawings made on the spot by
Major Koehler. According to the Corsican
accounts, the number of the French troops
amounted to about two thousand, to which
should be added the crews of four frigates.
He then observed, that with so small a land
force as that of the British, it would be fruit-
less to attempt a descent without the hearty
concurrence and aid of the Corsicans. But
with these, if the attempt was made instantly,
before the enemy were more prepared, there
was reason to hope for success. Should this
be resolved upon, he recommended that, for
the security of the fleet, possession should
first be taken of Martello bay; and he par-

ticularized the operations which would be requisite to accomplish this. Paoli had desired him also to signify that he required for his auxiliaries four thousand pounds, and a hundred barrels of gunpowder, to enable them to co-operate with the British.

It afterwards appeared that the Corsicans were grossly mistaken as to the numbers of the French, who had actually seven thousand men in arms in the different garrisons.

The whole of the report being approved of by the commanders, they sailed to Porto Ferrara to assemble the troops, and collect ordnance stores for the invasion. During this passage, the captain of the ship one night burst into the outer-cabin where General Dundas, Sir James St. Clair,* and Moore were lying; he exclaimed, ' Rise, gentlemen, for ' the ship is driving on a lee-shore :' he then passed into the inner cabin, and repeated the same alarming news to Lord Hood; adding, that he feared the ship would soon strike. Moore, from the position of his cot,

---

* The present Earl Rosslyn.

could see into Lord Hood's cabin, and he observed that his countenance was no way discomposed. He saw him also carefully draw on one pair of worsted hose over another, to protect his thin legs from the cold. This precaution tranquillised Moore, who being aware that a landsman could do nothing to avert the danger, remained in bed, and fell fast asleep. On awakening next morning he learned that the ship had weathered the lee-shore.

The fleet sailed to, and anchored at Porto Ferrara, where preparations were made for a descent on Corsica; but much delay occurred from the disordered state of the ordnance. At length the troops were embarked, and reached the Martello point on the 7th of February. On that evening, conformably to orders from General Dundas, Moore landed on the coast with six hundred and fifty soldiers, one hundred and fifty seamen, and two light guns. Early next morning he marched forward to turn and attack the enemy's works. It was with extreme diffi-

culty that the seamen and soldiers could drag
the guns over the rugged ground.   This, however, was effected, and he pushed on, with an
advanced party, getting into the rear of the
fortifications, which he carefully reconnoi-
tered.

He soon discovered that the three weeks
which had elapsed since he last examined
them had been busily employed by the French.
A large redoubt had been erected in front of
Martello, and well supplied with cannon.
The tower of Fornelli had also been strength-
ened by embrasures cut around, and furnished with artillery.. In addition to which,
there were low batteries, and in front, a strong
enclosed work, named the Convention Redoubt, had been erected, and also planted
with guns.   On viewing these formidable
entrenchments, Moore paused: for he perceived that if he proceeded as had been
planned, the detachment must be destroyed.
He sent for Major Koehler, who, having inspected the works, was of the same opinion;
he then wrote to Sir David Dundas the state

of things, and took up a secure position on
the heights.

The situation of the fleet was almost as
embarrassing as that of the army; for the
ships were anchored on the open coast, being
prevented from entering the bay by the Martello tower.   Lord Hood conceiving that this
might soon be silenced, ordered a line-of-
battle ship and a frigate to attack it.   These
ships anchored within point blank shot, and
cannonaded the tower; but the stone walls
being circular and of great thickness, threw
off the balls; while the two guns of the
tower (there were no more) swept the decks of
the men-of-war, and made fearful havoc.   At
last red-hot shot set fire to the line-of-battle
ship, on which both sheered off, to escape
conflagration.   As nothing could be done
against this tower by sea, a land battery was
erected; but the guns, being six-pounders, had
no effect.   An eighteen-pounder was then procured from the Victory, which battered the
walls, and the infantry firing continually into
the embrasure, the garrison, consisting of only

one midshipman and thirty-six men, surrendered. These few defied for a week the whole
British fleet. This Martello tower was the
first of that species of fortification, and the
model of many erected since.

 When General Dundas had inspected the
French fortifications, and found that they were
much too strong to be carried by assault with
the handful of British troops under his command, he was exceedingly at a loss how to
act; for the Corsicans, who had joined, could
be of no use in attacking works. Moore,
however, with Koehler, examined every place,
and especially a steep, rocky hill, about seven
hundred yards from the Convention redoubt.
This height had not been occupied by the
French, who deemed it impracticable to drag
cannon up so precipitous a crag. They knew
not the energies of British seamen, and Moore
recommended to the General to make that
attempt, which Sir David said he would try.
After two days hard labour, by the help of
blocks and ship-tackle, two eighteen-pounders
were hauled up, and mounted upon the top of

the rock, from whence the shot plunged into the redoubt. Another battery of smaller guns was also established upon a neighbouring eminence. In a couple of days some of the French cannon were dismounted, and the rampart shattered. The General then gave Moore orders to storm the redoubt. The troops were divided into three columns; a central one to advance in front, another to move on the right flank, and the Corsicans on the left, and to get into the rear to cut off the retreat of the French, in case of success.

Moore, placing himself at the head of the grenadiers of the centre column, advanced quickly and silently through the thick brush-wood by moonlight. When within fifty yards of the redoubt, he noticed that he was screened from the fire by the brow of the hill. He halted there for a few minutes, to give the men time to recover breath, and to restore their order, somewhat broken by hurrying over rough ground. Then, by his command, whose spirit was transfused to the soldiers, they rushed up the height and leaped into the entrenchment. The first traverse was carried; then he made for the second, and sprang to the embrasure, where a French gunner, who had a match in his hand, from some lucky chance, neglected to apply it to the cannon. A few soldiers followed Moore, but the enemy fired briskly, and charged with bayonets. The British, for the first time, began also to fire, and were fairly checked by the firmness of the enemy. They stepped back, yet without attempting to turn, and the bayonets of both crossed each other. While Moore was encouraging his men to break through, which he had no doubt they would have done, he heard voices in the rear crying out that there was another passage to the right; he immediately made for it and got in. He was encountered by a French soldier, and, evading his bayonet, made a thrust at him with his sword, which bent; but a second thrust instantaneously followed, which passed through his enemy's body. The British continued to pour in; some of the French fought bravely, and were bayonetted;

others threw down their arms, surrendering
themselves prisoners. A captain presented his
sword to Colonel Moore, and asked for quarter.
This was given, and he was directed to go
into the rear; when, finding himself in safety,
he exclaimed, ' Quel malheur pour un gallant
' homme qui voudroit se distinguer et s'élever,
' d'etre flanqué dans une fichue batterie com-
' me celle-ci!'

The column on the right, which had been
impeded by the difficulties of the ground,
now crowded also into the redoubt, strewed
with the wounded and the dying, and where
the victors and vanquished were mingled con-
fusedly. Hardly were the British masters
of the place, when grape-shot were fired upon
them from the tower of Fornelli; on which
Moore drew back the soldiers, entrenching
tools were employed, and abundance of sand-
bags being found in the redoubt, these were
arranged to cover the men. Before this was
effected, the firing ceased, as Fornelli was
evacuated.

The loss of the French in this storm was

about two hundred men. Had the Corsican column obeyed their orders, and advanced into the rear, not one of the fugitives could have escaped.

The capture of the Convention fort alarmed the French commander so much, that next day he evacuated the town of St. Fiorenzo, and all the neighbouring entrenched posts, and retreated towards Bastia. Paoli, with his Corsicans, had undertaken to interrupt this communication, but the Corsicans were unequal to opposing regular troops; they could only skirmish, or harass a retreating foe. By this failure Bastia received a numerous reinforcement to its garrison. After taking possession of St. Fiorenzo, General Dundas moved towards Bastia; but at the same time a sally was made by the French, who drove the Corsicans from a strong height, where they had been posted; which was the ground that General Dundas intended to occupy, as it was from that height alone that Bastia could be successfully assailed. This, together with the escape of the garrisons, were

serious disappointments, and the general had
now a better opportunity than before of learning the strength of Bastia. Before this fortress could be invested, it was necessary
that the French should be driven from the
high ground, where a strong detachment were
entrenching themselves. The ascent to this
was extremely difficult, and it could only be
taken by storm, which would occasion a great
loss of men, and the attack might fail. Were
it to succeed, batteries might be raised there;
but the ramparts of Bastia were protected by
strong redoubts, with abundance of artillery,
which could not be mastered without more
slaughter:—and the garrison could then retire
into the citadel, which commanded the town,
and would require another siege.

Added to these obstacles, the troops within
the town were far superior to the united British and Corsicans. On weighing these circumstances, General Dundas conceived it
would be extremely imprudent to attack
Bastia by force. But Lord Hood slighted all
his arguments and statements, yet advanced no

reasons in reply. Instead of which he made many bold assertions, and this among others, that six or seven shells thrown in would do the business of Bastia! Surely the compulsory retreat from Toulon might have instructed him to appreciate more justly French troops. But he was inflexible, and paying not the smallest respect to General Dundas, an able and experienced officer, he* dispatched three naval captains to Lieutenant-Colonels Moore and Villette, to know their opinions of the practicability of attacking Bastia; to which Moore instantly answered, that 'after his commander ' had declared that he considered it impracti- ' cable, it seemed to him a species of mutiny ' for a subordinate officer to deliver any opi- ' nion.' This mission not succeeding, Lord Hood wrote to General Dundas a letter, stating plainly, that ' upon the evacuation of ' Toulon, he conceived the general's command ' to have ceased, and from that moment he ' (Lord Hood) had the supreme command of

* From the M.S. Journal.

' the fleet and army, and it was from courtesy
' only that he had admitted the general to
' interfere.' The general answered this, by
thanking him, ironically, for his courtesy,
and by requesting him to show his commission
from the king, appointing him to the supreme
command of the army. The general then
assembled the commanding officers of corps,
to whom he read this correspondence, all of
whom agreed in considering Lord Hood's pre-
tension to command the army as unfounded,
and they resolved to resist any such attempt.
Sir David then informed the officers that some
months previously, on account of bad health,
he had written home for a successor, and that
he now resolved to quit the command, and to
return to England. In a few days after this,
he gave up the command to Brigadier-General
D'Aubant, an engineer officer who was next
in seniority. The brigadier's knowledge of
fortification made him even more averse than
General Dundas to undertake the siege of
Bastia. A strict blockade was all that he judged
proper to be established for the reduction of

the place, and the positions of the troops and
disposition of the Corsicans completely prevented the entrance of provisions by land.
Lord Hood, however, was so fixed in his own
notions, that he resolved to attack Bastia with
the marines of the fleet, and those troops who
had acted as marines. About seven or eight
hundred soldiers, which was about half the
British force, were then embarked, and the
command given to Lieutenant-Colonel Villette.
On the 2nd of April they sailed, and were landed
on the north side of the town. These troops,
together with a body of seamen under Captain
Nelson,[*] took post on a hill at a considerable
distance from the outworks, where they erected
batteries, and fired shot and shells, wasting
uselessly much ammunition. The enemy
paid little attention to this cannonade, only
returning a shot occasionally. But an event
of real importance occurred; a safe anchorage for the fleet, near the mouth of the harbour, was fortunately discovered; by which

---

[*] Afterwards Lord Nelson.

the entrance of victualling vessels into the town was rendered impracticable. The attack on the land side availed nothing; for the troops never durst approach beyond the parapet of their batteries on the summit of the hill. But famine at length was felt in the town, by which the garrison was compelled to capitulate on the 23rd of May. On that very day, an aide-de-camp of the French commander came over to the British advanced picket, and requested to speak to Colonel Moore. He told him that he had orders to deliver up the post in front of the English immediately, and therefore wished some troops to be sent to take possession of it.

Moore entered into conversation with this officer, who informed him, that there were six thousand men in arms in Bastia; four thousand five hundred of whom were well trained; consequently they never had the least apprehension of being taken by force, but that want of provisions compelled them to surrender.

A few days after this Moore was introduced to General Gentile, whom he asked, why, with his numerous garrison, he had never made one sally. He replied, 'Because no sally could bring us in bread.'

A short time before Bastia yielded, six hundred recruits arrived from Gibraltar; and soon after General Sir Charles Stuart came commissioned from England, to whom General D'Aubant resigned the command of the army.

CHAPTER V.

THE SIEGE OF CALVI—CORSICA WON AND LOST.

THE arrival of Sir Charles Stuart, who was endowed with superior military talents, was a most agreeable event to Lieutenant-Colonel Moore. A confidential and friendly intercourse was soon formed between them, and the General resolved upon undertaking the siege of Calvi, the only remaining place which the French possessed in Corsica. About this time General Trigge reached Bastia with eight hundred men, and was appointed to the command of that town. All the flank companies were then formed into one corps, denominated the reserve, the command of which was given to Moore; and the army, amounting only to about two thousand men, sailed in transports, and were landed, on the 29th of June, near Calvi, where they were joined by a body of Corsicans.

In the front of the town there was a strong stone fort, named the Mozello, and upon a rock towards the coast, another, flanking the first, called Mollinochesco. The town itself was surrounded with entrenchments, and had a garrison exceeding the British in numbers. This enterprise was a very arduous one: for independent of the strength of the fortifications, the town is situated in a marsh, where the ague is endemic, and the weather was then sultry and most oppressive to northern soldiers. The General perceived that, if he proceeded by regular approaches, sickness would waste down his force, and compel him to withdraw. Success could only be hoped for by daring and precipitate measures. He, therefore, pressed forward the landing of the ordnance, ammunition, stores and provisions; and not having sufficient means, he made repeated representations to Lord Hood for naval aid: at last fifty seamen were obtained, commanded by Captain Nelson,—re-

nowned subsequently for his glorious achieve-
ments.   While these preparatory measures
were advancing, the French were labouring
incessantly to strengthen their works; and
before the first battery was raised against
the Mollinochesco, they sallied forth, assisted
on their flank by a gun-boat, and attacked the
advanced Corsican post. The Corsicans fell
back, but the General dispatched Moore, with
some British light infantry and two field-
pieces, to their assistance, who, after a sharp
skirmish, repelled the French.

On July 4th, a battery opened against the
Mollinochesco, and preparations were made
to erect a strong breaching battery as near
as possible to the Mozello. The General
had fixed upon a spot within seven hundred
yards of the fort; and upon the success of
this operation the fate of the siege depended.
The attempt was made on the night of the
6th of July, and Sir Charles went himself to
see what progress was making: but found
that, owing to the negligence of an officer of
engineers, the battery could not be finished

before day-break : on which he ordered that the ground which had been broken up should be smoothed down for concealment, and the party retired undiscovered by the enemy.

Next night the attempt was resumed. On the approach of darkness a false attack was made on the Mollinochesco by the Corsicans, supported by a British regiment, and cannon fired incessantly. The French were so much alarmed on that side, that they surrounded themselves with light troops, dreading a serious assault, and fired briskly on that quarter. But as soon as it was quite dark, the reserve, followed by a working party, moved silently towards the ground where the failure had occurred the previous night. Moore advanced a line of soldiers in front, and made them lie down on their arms behind an enclosure. Under their protection a body of soldiers and sailors worked hard to raise an entrenchment, and to drag into it a heavy battering train with the necessary ammunition. To mislead the enemy, a small battery was also constructed on a more conspi-

cuous place at some distance in the rear.
This at dawn was first seen, and was fired at,
as was expected. But at six o'clock in the
morning, before the principal battery was
finished, the design was discovered, and immediately the French commenced a· furious
cannonade of round and grape shot intermixed
with shells from the Mozello fort, and from
redoubts on each flank. For two hours little
return could be made by the British : but
when the guns from the battery opened, the
enemy's fire was somewhat checked ; yet
during the whole of the day it had the
advantage. An English officer and a number
of men were killed and wounded, and two of
the battering guns were dismounted. When
night came, the enemy evacuated the Mollinochesco fort, which gave an opportunity to the
general to practise another feint. Some tents
were pitched there, as if it had been occupied
by troops, which attracted a portion of the
enemy's fire ; and in the course of the night,
the battery fronting the Mozello fort was re-

paired, the guns remounted, and traverses for their protection thrown up.

The general, who was both adventurous and indefatigable, passed the night with Moore in the work, to give encouragement and excite exertion. The cannonade never ceased, and when daylight appeared, became hot and so well aimed, that almost every shot struck the new-raised rampart. Bombs were also thrown in, and one blew up some cartridges and set on fire the fusees of a heap of shells, which burst in quick succession. The explosion was so tremendous, that Moore imagined some strange new-invented combustible engine had been thrown into the redoubt. The General received a blow from a splinter, but, what was quite marvellous, no person was materially hurt ; though the enemy, imagining that all in the rampart were blown to atoms, gave a shout of joy.

By degrees the fire from this breaching battery gained the superiority, and that of the enemy lessened. On July 10th, another battery, two hundred yards in advance, was erected, which silenced the guns of the Mozello; a brisk fire, *en ricochet*, however, opened from the town. One ball struck some stones, a splinter of which knocked down Moore's bat-man standing at his side, and some rubbish was dashed upon Captain Nelson's face, by which unfortunately he lost the vision of one eye.

As Sir Charles Stuart slept every night in the trenches, and reconnoitred the effects of the cannonade very frequently, Moore admonished him against exposing himself so much. His reply was, that he considered it the peculiar duty of the commander to examine personally the state of the breach, lest he should expose others to the more imminent danger of storming before it was practicable. This answer, characteristic of Sir Charles Stuart, was never effaced from Moore's memory.

On the 18th of July it appeared that the cannon had made an assailable opening in the rampart of the Mozello fort, and the following day was fixed upon for the storm. The troops were assembled at one in the morning, and arranged in three columns. The reserve was to assault the Mozello, a second column a work on the left; and the third to follow in the rear to give support wherever wanted. At dawn, Moore, at the head of the grenadiers of the reserve, marched to the breach under a heavy fire of cannon and musketry. They advanced with steady bravery to the palisades, which some artificers hastened to cut down. But before this could be effected, Moore and Captain Macdonald* got through an opening which had been made by shot, some soldiers followed, and giving a cheer, ran up to the breach. They were opposed by shot, by hand grenades, and by lighted shells rolled over from the rampart, which burst among the assailants. A fragment of one of these struck Moore on the head; he was whirled round, and for a minute stunned. On recovering

---

* Captain of the Royals, who was severely wounded.

his senses, he mounted the breach along with the grenadiers.

When Sir Charles Stuart, who watched the event with intense anxiety, saw the shells rolled down, and heard their explosion, he was much alarmed. But, on descrying the storming party with charged bayonets rushing into the fort, his trouble was changed into gladness. He ran towards the breach, climbed over the rubbish, and seeing Moore, whose face streamed with blood, surrounded by the grenadiers, huzzaing at having chased out the French, he caught him in his arms, and could hardly utter his fervid congratulations.

This important post being gained, new and powerful batteries were raised upon it; though the excessive heat of the weather, and the destructive sickness that prevailed, retarded the work: but when the guns opened, they made great havoc, and set the town on fire in different places. As no return could be made by the garrison, whose guns were silenced, a capitulation was signed on the 2nd of August, on terms dictated by Sir Charles.

By this time two-thirds of his troops were in the hospital, and officers and men were dropping down daily from sickness. If the town could have held out for another week, the siege must have been raised, from the ravage caused by the endemic fever.

The obstacles to success were surmounted chiefly by the talents, the energy, and valour of Sir Charles Stuart; and his disinterestedness at the conclusion was also remarkable. For he gave his share of the prize money, arising from the captured shipping and public stores, to be divided among the troops and the widows of the soldiers who had fallen in the contest: he also paid great attention to have the sick and wounded carefully tended, and settled the troops in good cantonments.

His acquaintance with Moore began on this occasion, and he continued henceforth one of his warmest friends. Yet he regretted that it was not in his power to bestow upon him any adequate reward for his services. But as Sir James St. Clair, the adjutant-general;

was about to return to England, Sir Charles pressed Moore to accept of his office, which might lead to further advancement.

In the government dispatches relative to the surrender of Calvi, the list of killed and wounded given in by the superintending surgeon was subjoined; but Captain Nelson's name was accidentally left out, as he had gone aboard his ship to be treated for his hurt by his own surgeon. Some weeks afterwards, when he read the printed gazette, he was highly offended at this trivial omission, but consoled himself by saying that 'one day he would have a gazette of his own.' This prophecy was frequently and gloriously fulfilled.

After the proper arrangements were settled, Sir Charles proposed to Colonel Moore their making a tour through the island, to gain a knowledge of the country, and of the manners and sentiments of the inhabitants. Sir James St. Clair, and two other officers, were invited to accompany them. In travelling from Calvi to the interior of the country their way lay through uncultivated grounds, and woods principally of the holm-oak. They slept the first night on the open field, although it rained the greatest part of the time; but the preceding campaign had hardened them. Next day, after a fatiguing journey, they reached Otta ; on approaching which village a number of the inhabitants came out to meet them, cheerfully shouting ' *Viva il Generale ! Vivano nostri Inglesi!* ' &c., and accompanied them to the house of their chief, the Signor Benedetti, who, together with his Signora, received them with much hospitality. The situation of Otta is singularly romantic, and the surrounding mountains magnificent. The hills in the vicinity are planted with vines, olives, and figs; which culture shows what great improvement might be made if the people were industrious. But they are averse to labour, and prefer living scantily, and strolling about with a gun listlessly.

On leaving Otta the travellers ascended a steep mountain, named Spelanca, and passed through several villages on the way to Vico.

The country around abounds with chestnut trees, the fruit of which is the principal food of the inhabitants. This district is considered healthy, probably more so than the coast; yet the pallid countenances of the Corsicans give an impression that no part of the island is salubrious. The General and his friends took up their abode in a convent of monks, who received them kindly. In this village the French formerly kept a detachment of troops, and the inhabitants expressed an ardent wish to have an English garrison, which astonished Sir Charles. But many sensible persons assured him, and he found it almost the universal opinion, that nothing but a military government would suit Corsica; as the people would submit to no other, and the laws could be enforced by no milder means. All around Vico there are extensive vineyards, and the wine is excellent.

The party next travelled to Ajaccio, by far the best town in the island. It is enclosed with a wall, and has a fortified citadel; but there is no water, except what is preserved in cisterns, an irremediable defect. Yet the harbour is good, and the town well adapted for commerce. The British officers were invited to the house of Signor Peraldi, a nobleman of distinction, who assembled the principal persons of the place to meet them, whose manners were altogether French, and the ladies more polite, and handsomer, than any they had before seen; they danced with them every night.

Benefaccio and Porto Vecchio were next visited; the latter is uninhabitable for half the year, from unwholesome vapours. While these prevail, the inhabitants retire to the neighbouring mountains. Corte, which is situated in the centre of the island, was lastly visited; it is considered the capital, and the Provisionary Council resided there, who entertained them; but they appeared to be persons of very little cultivation. Corte is a small town, with a cheerful aspect, surrounded by three rivers. From Corte the travellers returned to Bastia, on a road made by the French.

After their return an unpleasant collision
occurred between Sir Charles Stuart and Sir
Gilbert Elliot. The latter, not contented with
the civil authority, which in so disorganized
a country required abundant employment,
began to interfere with military matters. This
Sir Charles resisted, declaring to Sir Gilbert
that having been appointed Commander of
the British Forces he would yield him no
obedience, in any business respecting the
army, until Sir Gilbert had a commission
from the King, empowering him to command.
But on the 9th of October it was announced
officially that Sir Gilbert Elliot was appointed Viceroy, which astonished the Corsicans, who had neither recommended nor
contemplated such an appointment. Sir Gilbert now stood upon high ground, but did
not compose his difference with the General.
As an invasion from France was apprehended, it was judged expedient to raise a
corps of Corsican troops, and to place them
under the command of British officers. The
General considered the business maturely,

and presented a plan to the Viceroy, who, without the slightest regard to the General's opinion, altered it in a number of essential particulars, and appointed the officers without his recommendation.

Sir Charles, who possessed a lofty spirit, was indignant that a military plan meditated by him was rejected, and that his opinions for the defence of the island were unceremoniously set at nought by a person ignorant of such subjects. He would not for an instant endure this treatment; but sent in his resignation, and soon after returned to England.

The impression made on Colonel Moore by this event is thus noticed in his Journal* :—

‘ The departure of Sir Charles Stuart is a ‘ blow which the army feel severely. Never ‘ had a general gained more deservedly the ‘ affection and confidence of his troops. His ‘ absence will be most sensibly felt, if ever ‘ the French attempt a landing in this island. ‘ From a pretty general acquaintance among

---

* MS. Journal, vol. ii. p. 1.

' the Corsicans, I have many opportunities of
' knowing the high esteem they all have for
' General Stuart.'

The passion for inventing political constitutions was at this time rife in Europe, and
Sir Gilbert Elliot composed one for Corsica,
which was assented to by deputies assembled
from various parts of the island. The scheme
was an imitation of the British constitution,
whose complex and costly machinery was
imposed upon a poor semi-barbarous people,
who could not comprehend it, and with whose
habits and institutions it was discordant.

Their parliament was summoned on the 6th
of February, to meet at Bastia : thus trans-
ferring the seat of government from Corte
in the centre of the island to the sea-coast.
The inconvenience of this change to most of
the members in a country where the roads
are execrable, occasioned discontent   It was
natural that the conduct of the new and foreign governor should be scrutinized, especially as it was suspected that he had neglected their admired compatriot, Paoli.

The parliament commenced their proceedings by the election of a president, and General Paoli was instantly chosen by acclama-
tion. A rumour arose that this choice had
alarmed the Viceroy, which was augmented
by an order issued next day to stop the bag-
gage-waggons of a British regiment, which
were to have marched from Bastia to Corte.
Strange surmises were thus excited, and Paoli
received an intimation from a member of the
council to advise him strongly not to accept
the chair of president. The good old man
accordingly, to prevent any commotion and
to avoid giving umbrage to the Viceroy, declined the office, alleging, as an excuse, his
great age. This was a very inauspicious beginning, as the Corsicans regretted it exceedingly, from their warm attachment to Paoli.
An incident, which occurred soon afterwards,
tended to foment rising discontents. The
streets leading to the citadel being dirty, the
Viceroy directed that a party of the Corsican
battalion should be ordered to cleanse them.
It was represented to him that they might

object to this, but he continued peremptory,
and insisted on obedience. When the men
were assembled, and told what they were to
do, they in anger threw down the shovels,
and dispersed, saying, that ' they were en-
' listed for soldiers, and not for scavengers.'
This was passed over, but the battalion became afterwards very troublesome. The Viceroy, most unfortunately, could not perceive the
necessity of conciliating the Corsicans, or of
acting in unison with their feelings. Soon after
this, he made a visit to Ajaccio, when the officers of a Corsican corps resolved to give him
a ball. The hall of the municipality was '
chosen for that purpose, in which had been
placed a bust of Paoli. Some of the officers
assembled there to consult about the decora-
tions, when an aid-de-camp of the Viceroy,
pointing to the bust, asked, ' What business
' has that old charlatan here ?' He then pulled
down the bust, and threw it into a small closet,
where it was broken to pieces. This insult to
their revered chief was soon reported all over
Corsica: yet no punishment was inflicted

upon the officer, who remained attached to the person of the Viceroy. These proceedings, and others of an unpopular nature, gave deep concern to Colonel Moore, but he had no influence whatever with the Viceroy, who from the period of the rupture with Sir Charles Stuart had behaved with marked coldness towards his friend. Moore, therefore, occupied himself with his military duties, which were very important, as, from the movements of the French fleet in the Mediterranean, a descent on Corsica was expected. General Trigge, to whom a chief command had been for the first time confided, was a respectable, well-meaning man; he consulted Colonel Moore most confidentially on the proper defensive measures, who advised their examining the whole coast, and they made a tour for this purpose together.

There are few or no inns in Corsica, but in travelling through the country the hospitality of the inhabitants supplies this defect. When in the middle of the day they stood in need of refreshment, by the direction of their guide, without any recommendation, they rode up to the principal house of any village they reached. This was generally that of the magistrate or of the clergyman. In the evening they did the same, and were always received with the greatest civility, and everything produced which the village could afford. This consisted sometimes of a little meat; but often only of cheese, milk, bread, and wine. In the most remote parts inquiries were constantly made for General Stuart, and when he was to return; so great was the attachment felt by all the people towards him.

During this journey, and two others, in which Colonel Moore traversed almost every part of the island, he remarked that a great portion of Corsica was barren and un-cultivated, but many parts were beautiful and romantic: for there are mountainous and woody tracts, with rivers and torrents, which form exquisite scenery. The trees are chiefly the white oak, the ilex, the pine, the chestnut, and the olive; the myrtle and arbutus also grow wild in profusion. In many places vines are cultivated, and the wine is good; but there is a great deficiency of grain, for which chestnuts are the substitute.

The Corsicans are generally well made, but short in stature, ill-favoured and pallid; and are in a more barbarous state than the peasantry of almost any other part of Europe, except in the neighbouring island of Sardinia. Few of the women are good-looking, except at Ajaccio and Bastia, where there were some ladies both handsome and perfectly well-bred; in these towns French manners are prevalent.

The island is thinly peopled, and the inhabitants all live in towns or villages. No single house is to be seen in the country, which would be perilous; for family feuds are hereditary, and perpetuated. Revenge is even considered a duty; and sometimes many years after an injury has been received, vengeance is taken by a descendant. Individuals, therefore, consider themselves safe in proportion to the number of their kindred,

Every Corsican has a musket, which he carries on his shoulder even when he goes to
tillage, or to tend a flock of sheep; and if
provoked has no scruple in using it. The
government is too feeble and disorganized to
prevent this; and is seldom able to punish
any delinquents, even murderers. The
trades-people in general are very dishonest
in traffic, demanding in payment for goods
not what is just, but what the purchaser is
likely to pay. On one occasion Paoli happened to observe some British officers saun-
tering about the country. He advised them
against venturing without a guard, as their
epaulettes were so great a temptation, that
they might be shot on their account. The
only religion in the island is the Roman
Catholic, and the people are very bigoted.
Perhaps the absolution from crimes and
vices, too easily obtained from their priests,
may have prevented the moral benefits of
Christianity. Yet these wild people are won-
derfully attached and faithful to their chiefs;
in defence of whom they boldly encounter

dangers and sacrifice their lives. They greatly admired the valour of the British troops, which they had witnessed, and whose frank good-humour pleased them; and they often expressed gratitude for their aid in expelling the French. Moore was a con- spicuous favourite, because he was strong, hardy and active, both on foot and on horse- back. He slept on the ground, fed with them on chestnuts when necessary, and talked with them familiarly. By the free- dom of habitudes, and of conversation with the best company of both sexes, he learned that the nation generally entertained a strong aversion to their former tyrants, the French, and a warm attachment to the British. Had this been fostered by wise and generous treatment, Corsica might long have remained a portion of our empire.

The parliamentary representatives of so rude a race were unqualified for devising prudent measures. Yet taxes were urged on them by the Viceroy, passed by the majority, and Paoli was totally neglected. The crown which he had bestowed on Great Britain was repaid with ingratitude; and he retired to his native village in the mountains, excluded from public affairs.

Unpopular transactions, which hurt the feelings of the Corsicans, raised up dissensions in their parliament, and discontents throughout the country, which Moore lamented exceedingly. He occupied himself in concerting measures with General Trigge for the defence of the island in case of invasion, and lived in strict intimacy with the principal officers, especially with Colonel Hildebrand Oakes and Lord Huntley, who had arrived with a fine regiment of Highlanders. On one occasion, along with these two officers and Colonel Giampietre, he paid a visit of respect to Paoli; who received them politely, but poured out all his griefs. He expressed himself, however, with great moderation; but dreaded unhappy consequences from the irritation of his countrymen. His words and venerable appearance moved all: Moore beheld him with respect, endeavoured to console

him, and took his leave. Soon after this visit,
General Trigge sent for Moore, and expressed
great sorrow at being obliged to deliver a
message from the Viceroy, that his connexion with Corsicans inimical to his measures, and the countenance and support which
he gave them, made it impossible for him
to carry through the acts that were requisite :
that the Viceroy had represented this to the
Secretary of State at home, who, in reply,
had empowered him to dismiss Colonel Moore
from the island ; and unless he would promise
to break off all connexion with the people
who opposed him, and support his measures
as far as he could, he should enforce the power
given to him.

Moore expressed to the General great indignation at the Viceroy's having represented
to the Secretary of State, and consequently to
the King, what was utterly groundless ; and
added, that he would consider of what reply to
make. After reflecting, he returned to General Trigge, and requested him to say to the
Viceroy, that he felt much injured by his

having given to the Secretary of State a
representation of his conduct void of founda-
tion; and he thought, before taking such a
step, that he ought to have been apprized of it.
He now desired an interview to learn what part
of his conduct was objected to, and to have
an opportunity of replying in the presence
of General Trigge. The audience was appointed for the next day, when, accompanied
by the General, he met the Viceroy, and Mr.
North, the Secretary. The substance of the
conference was this :—The Viceroy, after
paying Colonel Moore many compliments as
an officer, complained of his having taken,
for what reason he knew not, a decided part
against his measures; and of his_influence
among the Corsicans being so great, that his
opposition rendered it impossible for him to
carry on the government. Then he added,
that if Colonel Moore would promise to be
no longer connected with his opponents, and
never to express sentiments of disapprobation
of any acts of his government, but, on the
contrary, give him his support, he would then

postpone the execution of the power vested in him, to send him from the island.

Moore, in reply, positively denied that he had ever taken any part in the politics of the country, and defied the Viceroy to point out one action of his, authorising him to make the representation which he had sent to the Secretary of State. As to the condition which was required, he said, that neither Sir Gilbert Elliot nor any man whatever had a right to exact from him a promise to approve of measures of which he was ignorant, and that were to be brought forward in future; and that no interested motive could induce him to come under such an engagement, which he thought unbecoming. The Viceroy then declared that he must execute the power given him.

Sir Gilbert was a practised speaker, and had the advantage of being in high office, and in the confidence of the ministers in England. But the elevation of Moore's mind would not suffer him, from any personal consideration, to submit to an arbitrary demand.

A few hours after this conference, General

Trigge, with expressions of great regret, transmitted the Viceroy's command, that Moore should leave the island in eight-and-forty hours.

· This expeditious departure was impracticeable; he, however, sailed for Leghorn in a week. Before setting off, he went to Corte, to take an affectionate leave of the 51st regiment, who declared towards him their unalterable esteem. The Corsican battalion which was quartered there waited upon him in a body, and the supreme council also paid him a respectful visit, to intimate their deep concern at his departure.

But an act more unjustifiable, even than the above, quickly succeeded. An intimation was sent to General Paoli, that he also should immediately leave the country. Moore, in his journal, observes on this most impolitic exilement, that* ' The great object of Sir Gilbert ' for a long time has been to bring this about. ' But I fear the consequence will be the ' reverse of what he expects. I think Gene-

* Journal, MS., vol. ii. p. 69.

' ral Paoli's presence curbed his countrymen,
' and prevented their acting with the vio-
' lence to which they were inclined from
' their dislike to the Viceroy and his mea-
' sures.   I think it probable that, upon Paoli's
' departure, there will be immediate confu-
' sion.'

The above prediction was soon fulfilled.
Tumults and revolt broke out in various
places, as reverence for government was reversed.   Sir Gilbert in vain issued proclamations, and marched troops to suppress them.
The good-will 'that the Corsicans felt for the
British made them unwilling to proceed to
open hostilities ; but their abhorrence of the
Viceroy surmounted that regard, and even
their hatred to the French.   The whole
island soon rose in insurrection ; a few
French troops landed, and the combined
forces surrounded Bastia.   In conclusion, Sir
Gilbert was driven from Corsica, and the
island was lost to Great Britain, and gained
by France, precisely in one year from the
expulsion of Paoli.

CHAPTER VI.

MOORE REPELS AN ACCUSATION—IS PROMOTED
TO THE RANK OF BRIGADIER-GENERAL.

A YOUNG Lieutenant-Colonel who is dismissed
from his employment abroad, and ordered
home on a charge of misconduct, is in an
embarrassing predicament; and this was
augmented in Moore's case by his accuser
being a Viceroy, and a friend of the Secretary of State, to whom the cognizance of
the business officially belonged. Yet it has
been shown that he braved the Viceroy;
positively denied the charge, and defied him
to the proof. In this defence it was not his
military abilities that were to be exerted, but
others of a different description. His feelings on the occasion were manifested in the
following letter written to his father.

' Florence, 13th October, 1795.

' My dear Father,

' If you have received the letter which
' I wrote to you from Bastia some days ago,
' it will prevent your surprise at the date of
' this. I have reason, however, to doubt if
' you will receive it.

' In consequence of a representation from
' Sir Gilbert Elliot to the Secretary of State,
' that I had taken a part in the politics of
' Corsica hostile to him, I received the
' King's order to return home; there to re-
' ceive his Majesty's further pleasure. I left
' Bastia accordingly upon the 9th, landed at
' Leghorn on the 10th, and arrived here yes-
' terday. I hope the day after to-morrow to
' be able to proceed to Cuxhaven, and expect
' to be in London the first or second week in
' November.

' I can enter into no particulars in a letter
' which goes by post. I have written to
' General Stuart. Be so good as to call upon
' him, and endeavour to be quiet till I see
' you. Do not commit me, for my line is

' already determined on. I do not think in
' my life I ever did an action unworthy of
' you or of myself, and least of all does my
' conscience tell me that I deserve blame in
' the affair which occasions my return. I
' can say no more. Remember me affection-
' ately to my mother, &c., and believe me,
' my dear father, your affectionate son,

'J. MOORE.'

In travelling over the mountains of the
Tyrol, Moore was much amused, and im-
pressed favourably with the character of the
Tyrolese. The remarks in his journal on passing over a part of Germany, which he had not
before seen, indicated perfect composure of
mind. At Cuxhaven, being detained by a
contrary wind, he was joined by his banished
friend Paoli, who informed him that, to shun
Bastia, he had taken shipping at Fiorenza;
but that Sir Gilbert had visited him there
twice, and poured out upon him much sooth-
ing flattery.

On the 20th of November, the wind becoming fair, Moore sailed from Cuxhaven, and reached his father's house in London in five days. His arrival never failed to bring joy to his family; nor was this damped by the cause of his return,—for even his mother scorned an accusation brought against her son.

His first visit was to Mr. Pitt, the prime minister, who received him, as he imagined, with some stateliness. Mr. Pitt signified that the statements made by Sir Gilbert Elliot were so strong, that it was impossible for the ministers not to acquiesce in his recall, although they did so with regret; and that he should be happy to hear his justification, as no officer's character stood higher. Moore replied,—*'Corsica is the place where I should ' have been tried; there are the witnesses of ' my conduct; and I must represent to you, ' that I have been deprived of my situation ' without a trial. Here, I have nothing to ' offer against Sir Gilbert's representations but

---

* Journal, MS., vol. ii. p. 74.

' a complete denial of them, and to reply that
' he has been instigated by private malice to
' state what is utterly false ; and unless I am
' immediately employed, or have some mark of
' His Majesty's favour, as a proof to the army
' that my conduct was not disapproved of,
' I shall feel myself injured.' He spoke with
great warmth ; and on his intimacy with
persons hostile to Sir Gilbert being adverted
to, he said promptly, * ' Had I associated with
' such only who approved of Sir Gilbert's
' measures, I must have lived alone ; for I
' know no persons, Britons or Corsicans, ex-
' cepting those in his immediate pay, who did
' approve of them.'

Mr. Pitt finally told him to wait upon the
Duke of Portland, whose peculiar business this was: and he advised him not to
speak to his Grace the language of passion,
but to say everything he considered requisite,
calmly. It is well known that the Duke was
the intimate friend of Sir Gilbert Elliot, and

---

* Journal, MS.

it was generally understood that it was chiefly through his influence that His Grace had abandoned the parliamentary opposition, and accepted his present office. These were unfavourable circumstances. When Moore was introduced to the Duke, he presented the order he had received for his return, and said, that he now appeared to receive His Majesty's further pleasure.

The Duke paid him some compliments; but added, * ' That the confidence reposed in ' Sir Gilbert Elliot's situation rendered it ' impossible for ministers not to comply with ' his request,—as officially they must suppose ' him in the right; but that the matter no way ' affected his military character.'

The Duke's manners were polite and obliging. Moore observed,* ' If the recall has ' not affected my military character, it how- ' ever has affected essentially my military ' situation. And that it was treating an ' officer of my rank rather cavalierly, to dis-

* Journal, MS.

' miss him upon such general grounds without
' a trial. I felt the insult, and did expect
' immediate employment, as a reparation of
' the injury done to me, and a mark of the
' King's approbation.' He then argued on the
accusation ; and His Grace was either silent,
or repeated what he had before said, and
appeared much embarrassed.

His next interview was with Mr. Dundas,* who received him well, and after
hearing him, spoke out frankly. He said,
that Sir Gilbert on several occasions had
displayed a degree of jealousy he had not
thought him capable of; and then assured
Moore, that what had happened did not affect
his character in any respect, and if he wished
for employment he should be employed.

Mr. Dundas also informed him that Mr.
Pitt had spoken very favourably of him, and
had said that Moore had been harshly
treated, and his wish was that he should be
employed.

---

* Afterwards Lord Melville.

Moore likewise learned that the Duke of York had written to Sir William Fawcet,* that he was surprised at Sir Gilbert Elliot's conduct, and was determined to speak to the King about employing Moore immediately. The result was, that he was suddenly advanced to the rank of Brigadier-General in the West Indies; a promotion which far exceeded his hopes, and was ample atonement for his wrongs. This was the first occasion in which Moore had any intercourse with the ministers. It brought forth some display of the strength of his character; and from that period he was always favoured by Mr. Pitt. Thus by the very means designed for his depression, he wrought out a way to fame.

The brigade which he was appointed to command was then assembling at the Isle of Wight, and he joined it after four weeks' stay in London; for the urgency of the war prevented his parents and his family ever enjoying, for more than short intervals,

* Sir William Fawcet was Adjutant-General, and there being no Commander-in-Chief, had great sway.

after long absences, his much-loved society. His brigade consisted of foreign corps, chiefly French emigrant loyalists, who had been driven from their native country by the san-guinary revolution. The officers were highly polished and honourable men, whose society he found very agreeable.

In the beginning of the year 1796, the West Indies were thrown into a lamentable condition by the pseudo-philosophic decrees of the National Assembly of France. These false philanthropists, reckless of the ruin of their fellow-subjects, roused up the negroes, who perpetrated the most barbarous atrocities on the whole white population. In the French portion of St. Domingo hardly a white human being was left alive. St. Lucia was desolated; and the negroes in the other colonies were in arms. These horrors spread to the British islands. In Jamaica, the Maroons had revolted. In St. Vincent, the Negroes and Charibs were murdering every white man or woman that fell into their hands; and a revolt had also burst out in

Grenada. It was therefore judged requisite
to send an army under Sir Ralph Abercrombie for the preservation of our own
islands, and to subdue, if possible, some of
those appertaining to our enemies. A fleet,
consisting of above a hundred sail of transports with troops and stores, and a strong
convoy of men-of-war, commanded by Admiral Cornwallis, took their departure from
Spithead on the 28th of February. Moore,
with the foreign brigade, was in this fleet.
In sailing down the channel, with a fair wind,
a disastrous accident occurred, not unfrequent
in large fleets. The Admiral's ship ran
down and sunk a transport full of troops;
by which one hundred soldiers, half the com-
plement, were unhappily drowned.

Part of the fleet having reached Barbadoes
on the 15th of April, Moore waited on the
Commander-in-Chief, Sir Ralph Abercrombie, who received him with cordiality, and
conversed with him on the objects he had
in view with great openness. His duties
were multifarious; and both the British and

French islands being in combustion, it required sound judgment to dispose of the forces to the best advantage.

In the following day two strong detachments, including some of the foreign corps, were ordered to sail to St. Domingo, and another to Demerara and Berbice ; but Moore's name was not mentioned. On perceiving this, he again waited on Sir Ralph to learn his destination. Some conversation arose, when Moore said, that he was ready to go wherever he pleased, but was most desirous of commanding a brigade with the body of the army under him. This was exactly what Sir Ralph wished ; so he replied, that he would with pleasure agree to his request, and would always be happy to do what was agreeable to him. Moore, on leaving England, knowing that his friend Anderson, who had served with him in the 51st regiment, had sailed in this expedition for the West Indies, kept the situation of Brigade-Major open ; and conferred on him the appointment as soon as he arrived at Barbadoes.

. On the 22d of April the army was reimbarked, and sailed to attack the island of St. Lucia. That island is mountainous, remarkably strong by nature, and had been fortified by skilful French engineers. There rises from the sea, near the harbour, a high hill called Morne Fortuné, on which a strong fortress had been constructed. And at the basis of the hill along the beach, and on an island called Pigeon Island, there was a range of batteries, rendering it dangerous for ships to approach the shore.

It was resolved that a body of troops should be landed in a bay, called Ance le Cap, situated at some distance on the right of the Morne Fortuné, and that these should march round to get into the rear, and storm the sea batteries. Sir Ralph had promised Moore to give him employment, and he kept his word on this the first opportunity. He placed a corps of nineteen hundred men, for this operation, under the orders of Major-General Campbell; the first division of which, under Moore, was commanded to effect the landing. Some ships of war were directed by Admiral Christian to aid the troops; but in maritime expeditions great uncertainty occurs, as a variety of incalculable accidents often frustrate co-operations. On the present occasion some of the ships were blown to leeward; a line-of-battle ship got on shore, and an ordnance sloop was lost. In consequence of these untoward accidents, the transports which contained two regiments alone reached the bay in the morning, while the others were still at a considerable distance. But as the enemy, who had begun to fire at the shipping, were now apprised of the design, and would speedily be augmented, Moore landed at once with the 42nd Highlanders, and took up a good position, to cover the remaining disembarkation. He was assailed, and skirmished for some hours with parties of the enemy, keeping them at bay. Before noon, General Campbell came ashore, and informed Moore, that the whole of the troops could not be landed until the evening, and that orders had been received from Sir

Ralph to postpone the descent altogether, as
the Admiral was not ready to co-operate. This
counter-order came too late; for Moore considered that it would be both dangerous and
disgraceful to retire and reimbark in the face
of the enemy. He, therefore, prevailed upon
General Campbell to send an officer to Sir
Ralph, to explain their situation; and to
obtain leave to march forward in the night,
to turn the enemies' batteries at Trovillac and
Brelotte. Sir Ralph, confiding in the representation, sent back permission to act as
they judged best. General Campbell, who
was extremely ill, then begged Moore to issue
the proper orders for the march. In the
course of that evening, the other regiments of
the detachment landed on the beach, and
made their junction. At three o'clock in the
morning they moved forward in a long column, by moonlight, and soon fell in with a
party of the enemy, who fired upon them
and fled; then, without further opposition,
they reached the heights above Choke bay.
This movement so alarmed the enemy, that

they evacuated their batteries on the shore and retired; notice of which having been sent to the Admiral, the fleet stood in and anchored, and the troops on board landed undisturbed. Sir Ralph, with his staff, proceeded to the heights where Moore was posted; and having ordered a company of grenadiers to drive back a picket of the enemy, he went forward to reconnoitre the grounds around with Moore, who writes, ' Sir Ralph is very short-sighted; without a ' glass he sees nothing, but with one he ob- ' serves ground quick and well. He has the ' real eagerness of youth, and for his age has ' much activity of body and mind.' After this inspection it appeared to the General, that the preferable course for investing the Morne Fortuné was to march a body of troops into the country, who should ascend another high hill, named the Morne Chabot, situated behind the former. It was foreseen that this would be a very hazardous enterprise, as Morne Chabot was occupied by the enemy. Sir Ralph, however, resolved to attempt it; and on returning, gave orders that Brigadier Moore, with a column of a thousand men, should march at twelve o'clock at night, and that *Brigadier Hope should follow an hour afterwards, with another column of the same number, to drive the enemy from Morne Chabot. This sudden call for fresh exertions, left Moore little time to repose from the fatigues already undergone. At half-past eleven at night, he paraded the troops and concerted with General Hope, that he should march on first until he reached the foot of the hill, there halt, and wait for Hope's arrival; and that at dawn both should simultaneously storm the Morne. He moved off precisely at midnight, the grenadiers and light infantry heading the column. The road was much broken, and so narrow, that in many places there was only space for marching in a single file. The moon, however, shone bright, and he pushed forward. At about four in the

* Afterwards Earl Hopetoun.

morning, when traversing a thick wood, the
advanced party was challenged and fired at;
a number of voices were then heard, and more
shots succeeded, on which the party, according to orders, fell back.   A soldier who was
killed, in falling caught hold of Brigade-
Major Anderson, and both rolled down a de-
clivity; but Anderson soon rose, and returned to the front.   The plan of lying concealed, and of attacking in conjunction with
Brigadier Hope, was thus frustrated; for
Moore thought that to remain waiting in file,
in an unknown wood, would be much more
perilous than to attack alone; therefore, without a moment's hesitation, he gave orders to
advance, and the path soon widened sufficiently to admit seven men in front.   The
enemy's picket, consisting of about fifty men,
fired a volley; some men fell, but the rest
advanced, and drove off the enemy.   Moore
quickly arranged the grenadiers on the ground
on which the enemy's picket had been posted,
and the light infantry were drawn up to cover
them.   Then leaving orders for the rest of
the column, as it came up, to form on that

spot, and follow, he exhorted the grenadiers not to fire, but to advance and use their bayonets. They were soon stopped by a strong fence, which he directed them to pull down, but this they could not do with all their strength; he then commanded them to leap over it, and on their hesitating, showed them the example, which they followed. The enemy, who crowned the hill above them, fired with great effect; and, notwithstanding all Moore's efforts, he could not prevent his soldiers from returning the fire, and induce them to advance with their bayonets. They received repeated discharges from above, within twenty or thirty yards, and as his men in the rear began also to fire, no situation could be more distressing. The grenadiers and light infantry, though much disordered, continued however advancing slowly; and Moore was hoarse and exhausted with calling to them ' Forward! we have almost ' gained the heights!' with similar exhortations. At last they reached the summit of the hill, and bayonetted such of their enemies as had not time to escape.

In this attack, a grenadier, who had thrust himself forward, received a ball levelled at Moore, and fell dead in his arms. His Brigade-Major, Anderson, as he was gallantly encouraging the soldiers to mount the hill, was severely wounded in the side. The loss in this conflict fell heavily on the grenadiers and light infantry of the 53rd regiment, who fought bravely, being commanded by the General's son, Lieutenant-Colonel Abercrombie. Not one of them drew back, though under a most heavy fire. Had they given way, the whole column might have been thrown into disorder, and carnage and discomfiture would have ensued. Moore, who was keenly sensible of this, wrote—' I don't ' know that I ever felt more satisfaction than ' upon gaining the heights ; I had almost de-' spaired of it. The consequences of a failure ' were strongly imprinted on my mind *.' General Hope, on his march, heard the firing, and hastened on with ardour to participate

* MS. Journal, vol. iii. p. 21.

in the danger, but could not reach the basis of the hill until the summit was gained. When he had brought up his column to Morne Chabot, he and Moore reconnoitred the place, and they observed another hill extremely commanding, called Morne de Chasseau, the possession of which would greatly facilitate the approaches to Morne Fortuné. As officers when detached should employ their judgment, and act according to the spirit of their orders, rather than adhere to a literal obedience, Moore determined to seize upon Morne de Chasseau immediately, before the enemy could recover from their panic. Accordingly, along with General Hope, he marched to the top of that hill, posted there a strong detachment, and threw forward pickets to within twelve hundred yards of the entrenchments on Morne Fortuné.

The next day Sir Ralph visited Moore on his post, shook him by the hand, thanked him warmly, and highly approved of all he had done.

While the enemy's attention was entirely
turned towards this quarter, Major-General
Morshead quietly landed a considerable
body of troops under his command to the
left of the fortress, and Sir Ralph, being very
desirous of getting possession of the sea batteries at the basis of Morne Fortuné, made a
disposition to storm them, chiefly by this
reinforcement; but as General Morshead fell
sick, the command devolved upon another
officer. The troops were formed into columns, one to attack a battery on the left,
and the principal corps to storm that on the
centre: and a third column, under General
Hope, was ordered to move down from Morne
Chabot, to attack the battery on the right.
The whole moved off at midnight to avoid
cannon shot; and before day-break, General
Hope, with his usual bravery, carried the
work against which he was directed. The
column on the left, commanded by Colonel
Riddle, had equal success; but the central
column, from some unexplained cause, never
came into action. The two other corps,

therefore, remained unsupported, and were, in the military phrase, in the air. At day-light they were furiously cannonaded from the fortress above, and, being attacked by the enemy's whole force, were constrained to return with considerable loss to their former positions.

Sir Ralph was much disappointed by this failure, but did not renew the design. Instead of which, he extended General Morshead's division around the back of the Morne Fortuné, in a chain of posts reaching to Morne de Chasseau; and thus cut off the enemy's communication with the interior of the country.

Sir Ralph then determined to make his approaches from Moore's post at Morne de Chasseau, and ordered a road to be made in that direction for dragging up cannon and ordnance stores. A party of seamen also were landed to give their assistance in this laborious work, and in erecting batteries on the heights. To intercept these operations, the enemy made frequent sallies, skirmishing with the pickets, and the fire from the outworks gave great annoyance. The work, however, proceeded; sixteen pieces of ordnance were mounted on the batteries, which opened on the 16th of May. As the distance to the Morne Fortuné was great, the fire had less effect than was expected, and was briskly returned. The guns, indeed, were so ill-directed, that after cannonading two days, a cannon in an advanced outwork, not six hundred yards distant, was not dismounted. But Moore observing that the men were compelled to hide themselves, on the reverse of the hill, ordered fifty soldiers, supported by double that number, to ascend by a concealed path, and carry the work. To prevent their being discovered, a twelve-pounder was fired constantly until the first party were near the entrenchment, into which they rushed, bayonetted some of the enemy, and drove out the rest. The gun was then spiked and thrown down the hill, and the party returned without the loss of a man. On examining the place, Moore found it too much exposed to occupy it, but he established a post for a battery on an eminence less forward, but two hundred yards in front of the other batteries. By the same manœuvre, another harassing gun in the flank was spiked; but the officer who commanded rashly advanced too far, which brought on a sharp skirmish with a strong party of the French, who were at length repelled.

On the same night an unsuccessful attack was made on another point. There stretches out, on the right side of the harbour, a peninsula with a narrow neck, named the Vijie; the ground gradually rises, and was fortified. As this work commanded the principal anchorage, Sir Ralph was desirous of getting possession of the place, and ordered a regiment to assault it. The soldiers advanced with spirit, and carried the first battery; but a shower of grape-shot from a second threw them into confusion, and they took to flight; after which the design of attacking the Vijie was given up.

On the 18th, Sir Ralph came to Du Chasseau, and appeared much chagrined both at

the above repulse, and also at the slight effect
produced upon the enemy's entrenchments
by his batteries.   From the experience Moore
had acquired at the siege of Calvi, he sug-
gested that guns of a larger calibre should be
employed, and pushed nearer ;   accordingly
some twenty-four pounders were ordered to
be dragged up to the most advanced post, as
soon as the road was made practicable.   More
troops were also encamped around, as it was
intended that the approaches against the fortress should be made from that quarter.
Moore then found that, with all his vigilance,
he could not sufficiently superintend the
various posts, working parties, and nightly
watches under his direction ; he therefore
signified to Sir Ralph's aide-de-camp that he
wished General Knox to be appointed to take
a part of the duty.   Sir Ralph went up, took
Moore aside, and told him that he had never
thought of sending any one to supersede him,
and he was much surprised to learn that he
had applied for an officer his senior in rank.
To this Moore answered, ' I have asked for

' another General, because another is requi-
' site for the numerous duties. I ventured to
' propose General Knox, because he is a man
' of good sense and an excellent officer : for it
' is of the utmost importance that the service
' should be well conducted, but of none which
' of us commands.' The novelty of this senti-
ment surprised Sir Ralph, and when it was
divulged to the army, it excited amazement.
Next day, however, General Knox was put
in orders, and he and Moore acted in perfect
harmony.

On the morning of May 24th two new batteries, with twenty-four pound cannon, together with all the other batteries, opened upon
the fortress. In the front there was an advanced outwork, named a Flêche*, full of
troops. Some guns were directed against it ;
and after battering it for some hours, Moore
moved forward with the grenadiers and light
infantry of the 27th regiment, and carried the
work by storm. But no sooner had he driven

* Or Arrow, an angular work not inclosed.

out the enemy than a shower of grape-shot was poured upon him from the Morne Fortuné, only five hundred yards distant. Having determined to keep possession of the flèche, he ordered the soldiers to reverse the parapet, and to raise a trench to cover the flanks of the rest of the regiment, which came up to their aid. While working with the spade and pickaxe, under a heavy cannonade, a numerous body of the enemy sallied forth, who had the means of covering themselves by some houses, and by the inequalities of the ground; and their fire was deadly. Moore ordered the flank companies to charge, and drive them back. Colonel Drummond gallantly led them on. He engaged with his sword a French officer, whom he killed; and the enemy was repulsed by bayonets. But these brave troops, in returning to the flèche, suffered much from grape-shot fired from the batteries.

The French Governor, seeing this advantage, reinforced his party, and impelled them to make another sally with greater resolution,

They advanced boldly close up to the British, who, from the confined nature of the ground, could present only a narrow front. The enemy's fire was, consequently, superior, officers and men were falling fast, and Moore apprehended every instant that the regiment would give way. In this distress, two companies were again ordered to charge, which was done daringly; but Major Wilson and Captain Dunlop fell wounded, and many valiant soldiers were killed in this assault. Yet the others, undismayed, drove their enemies before the points of their bayonets, and pursued them with great slaughter to the fort. They were then recalled, but when retreating, exposed, as before, to the guns of the rampart. Moore then commanded the houses in front to be set fire to, and the entrenching to be proceeded in. He rallied his few remaining soldiers, and prepared them to repel a third sally, which he momentarily expected. But the fire from the enemy's cannon ceased, and when the smoke was dispersed, instead of an armed band of soldiers, there issued from the gate of the fortress a train of negro bearers carrying biers, to collect and take in the wounded, who, moaning piteously and crying for help, were strewed among heaps of the dead.

This havoc had daunted the enemy, and turned their thoughts from further fighting; and the mournful procession and melancholy occupation of the bearers was a conclusive proof of discomfiture.

Entrenching tools only were then wielded to erect a powerful battery in the Flêche, which had been won at such expense of blood.

These conflicts had been clearly seen, both by the besieged from Morne Fortuné, and by the besiegers from Morne de Chasseau, as from an amphitheatre. Sir Ralph stood in the centre battery, and viewed the whole with deep interest. When all was over, Moore went up to him to make his report, and attributed the success to the valour of the 27th regiment. The General ardently clasped his hand, and said, 'he could never ' requite the obligations he felt for his efforts ' on that day.'

The spirits of the besieged were so completely sunk by their defeat, that before night they sent out a flag of truce to solicit a suspension of hostilities; and next day their commander capitulated. The survivors of the garrison, amounting to two thousand men, most of whom were negroes and mulattoes, marched out of the works, and laid down their arms: when Moore took possession of the citadel with his division, at the head of which was the 27th regiment, whose colours were planted on the ramparts.

Sir Ralph immediately appointed him Commandant and Governor of St. Lucia, an office he accepted with extreme reluctance, as he would have greatly preferred continuing to serve with the principal army. But the General pressed it, on the grounds that his talents were necessary for the complete subjugation of the island. He also promoted Captain Anderson to the 31st regiment, who continued, notwithstanding, to act in Moore's staff as before.

CHAPTER VII.

BRIGADIER GENERAL MOORE, GOVERNOR OF ST. LUCIA—CONQUEST OF THE ISLAND—THE YELLOW FEVER.

ON June 4th Sir Ralph Abercrombie sailed with the army, escorted by a fleet commanded by Sir Hugh Christian, to reduce the revolted islands of Grenada and St. Vincent, and left Moore invested with the military power and civil administration of St. Lucia. Although the Morne Fortuné, and the posts adjoining the harbour, had been captured, the rest of the island remained unsubdued; the woods and fastnesses were filled with armed negroes and mulattoes; and multitudes of the prisoners, after the capitulation, being ill guarded, escaped and joined them.

The French agents, who had been sent forth to the West Indies during the frenzy of the revolution, were sanguinary men from

Paris, a city then resembling Rome in the reign of Nero, ' quo cuncta undique atrocia, ' aut pudenda confluunt, celebranturque *.'

The negroes and mulattoes, who acquired the name of Brigands, were armed, and declared free by those political fanatics, whose frantic decrees and atrocious exhortations kindled their fury to the height. Indeed, the ferocity of these emancipated slaves became direful. They threw off all compunctions of humanity to put on the savage nature of the wildest animals. A resolution to defend their liberties would neither have been unnatural, nor reprehensible, but this was sullied by deeds too horrible to be related.

The corporal frame and mental qualities of the negroes fit them peculiarly for desultory warfare. They are stout, agile, expert in the use of arms, and can endure patiently the scorching sun, and the torrents of rain of the tropical climate. They can live on the roots which grow spontaneously, or with little cul-

---

* ' Where all atrocities and pollutions are assembled and perpetrated.'—*Tacit.* lib. xv.

ture, in the fields; and being bold and cun-
ning are ready to oppose their enemies by
force, or to deceive them by stratagem. With
brutal fury they had murdered many of the
white inhabitants, sparing neither women nor
children; and those who remained alive had
fled for safety into the towns. But none of the
survivors, nor of the slaves who had continued
faithful to their masters, durst give any intelligence to, or have any communication with
the British: and Victor Hughes, the French
Commandant of Guadaloupe, contrived, in
spite of the British fleet, to send by small
vessels frequent supplies of arms, ammunition, and provisions, to these ferocious Brigands.

The British troops, who had been left
with Moore to contend with all these difficulties, were chiefly recruits, with inexperienced officers; for the jealousy of parliament against a standing army hinders such a
military force being kept up in peace as
would form the basis of a good army at the
commencement of war: therefore, when this

breaks out, sudden levies, at a vast expense, are enlisted; and the raw recruits, ignorant of their business, and without the habits of soldiers, are sent out on foreign service. From the same cause the various military departments were inefficient; even their chiefs were totally inexperienced on occasions where men of great resource, and capable of uncommon exertions, were wanted.

The negroes in St. Lucia had not only been active in deeds of cruelty, but in every species of villany. The conflagration of houses had been so extensive that there were not sufficient buildings remaining to shelter the troops, or even for an hospital; and the rainy season having set in, great sickness already prevailed. Altogether, the condition of the island was lamentable; but Moore struggled against the difficulties with all his faculties. One of his first measures was to publish a proclamation to the inhabitants, granting pardon to all who would come within the British lines, and deliver up their arms. Passes were also given to whoever wished to

return to their habitations, and all were promised protection, if they remained quietly
attending to their private affairs. Royalists
and Republicans were exhorted to refrain
from mutual recriminations, as both should
be treated with indulgence, and have equal
justice.

. The Brigands were not, however, to be
quelled by pacific measures ; intelligence was
brought daily to the Government House that
they were laying waste the country, and so-
licitations were made for soldiers to protect the
plantations ; but as the detaching troops in
separate bodies was a hazardous measure, the
Governor judged it expedient, before he came
to a decision, to make an excursion, and visit
the four largest towns,—Souffrieré, Choiseul,
Laborie, and Vieux Fort. In these places
he had an opportunity of conversing with the
principal people of the country, whom fear
had driven thither. He addressed them at
public meetings, encouraged them to return
to their estates, and gave assurances that
troops should be posted to protect their plan-

tations. He recommended them strongly to treat their slaves not only with lenity, but with kindness,—as men who had borne arms, and had been told they were free, would not without reluctance return to slavery and labour: but that, if those in the woods saw the others on the plantations well fed, comfortable, and happy, they might be induced to join them. That no harshness ought to be employed; as all mankind, of whatever colour, were entitled to justice, and would meet with it from him indiscriminately.

The spirit of the instructions from Sir Ralph Abercrombie was of a defensive nature, for he imagined that, by guarding the Morne Fortuné and the harbour, the sovereignty of the island would be preserved. But from personal inspection, and mature consideration, Moore was convinced that if this plan were adopted the whole country would quickly be devastated, and the negroes and men of colour would universally rise up and occupy the woods and eminences around the fort. He would then be environed, and in a manner besieged in a most unwholesome spot, where his troops would melt away so rapidly by disease that he would be forced to abandon the island altogether. These consequences appeared so certain, that he resolved to follow an opposite scheme,—to establish a line of posts for the protection of the plantations, and to act offensively by attacking the Brigands wherever he could find them, and compel them, if possible, to surrender their arms and live in peace.

Some few known agitators were then arrested, the principal of whom, Rupez Roche, had been one of the Republican agents. He possessed some property, was clever and ambitious, and had been active in stirring up the negroes. When sent for he protested that he was innocent, and confiding in his eloquence for his defence, he declaimed with theatrical gestures. But certain information had been procured of his communicating with the Brigands. He was told that he should be tried, and was ordered into confinement.

Some others, whose turbulent conduct was notorious, were shipped off from the island.

After having carefully examined the country, Moore marked out, towards the foot of the mountains, proper spots for the establishment of a line of posts to protect the principal plantations from the Brigands, who lurked in the mountains, which were covered with wood, and thence issued out to burn the dwellings, and to plunder and murder the inhabitants.

The coast was also guarded by detachments, for the important object of preventing supplies being sent to the enemy by sea. Orders were given to the officers to patrole from post to post for mutual aid, and to send in parties occasionally to scour the woods. Vigilance and strict discipline were also strongly inculcated. Before these measures were arranged, intelligence was received that a body of Brigands had approached near to Prasline, on which a corps was sent to occupy that place. The detachment, which amounted to eighty men, was attacked three

times by near three hundred Brigands, who
were repulsed, with the loss of twenty or
thirty. .

Moore was, however, much dissatisfied with
the officer for not charging boldly this as-
semblage,—an opportunity which he thought
ought not to have been lost. About the same
time he himself marched forward in the night
to drive some corps of Brigands from the
plantations near Dauphin. But on his approach they set fire to some houses, and fled
away, and neither by rewards nor threats
could any negro be induced to give the
least information of the route the enemy had
taken, so apprehensive were all of being
afterwards murdered. Indeed, the conduct
of the negroes, even to each other, was merciless, for they put to death, without hesitation, all men and women who refused to join
them. A guard was left at Dauphin, and he
proceeded to Demarie. On the way he
mounted a height, and saw the whole country
on fire, and a few negroes running off.
Some women then approached, begging pro-

tection. They said they had been in the woods, that their houses were burnt, and they had narrowly escaped with their lives.

When a few of his men were next day collecting cattle, they were assailed by a party of Brigands who rushed out upon them from a neighbouring wood. The soldiers fell back; but when the Brigands had swept together a quantity of cattle and other provisions, Moore advanced upon them, recovered the booty, and chased them to the mountains. He then marched towards Prasline, and learnt on the route that some companies of his black corps had defeated a party of the enemy. The black corps were indeed found the very best troops for that country; for the heat of the sun did not distress them; and they could march with much greater celerity than the British soldiers. He had occasion when near Prasline to reconnoitre a post, and was accompanied by an escort of only twenty men. In passing a river he was fired at by a party in the rear. No notice was taken of this, and he continued his march, which the

Brigands mistook for a flight, and they pursued with loud shouts. They amounted to about a hundred, of whom one-fourth had muskets, and the remainder pikes and other weapons. When they came pretty close, Moore ordered his men to halt, face about, fire a volley, and charge with bayonets. The Brigands had not firmness to resist this, they ran off, and left their ammunition boxes. In this affair it was only by great exertions that he could prevail on the soldiers to make the charge, as they were alarmed at the numbers of the enemy.

He then went to Vieux Fort, and formed a plan to surprise a camp of the Brigands on Morne Forcieuse. This would have completely succeeded, when a musket accidentally going off, gave the alarm, on which the enemy fled and dispersed; however, twenty or thirty were killed, and the camp burned.

In another quarter, by shameful negligence, a small British post was carried, and twelve soldiers killed and wounded; and, although the firing was heard at the neighbouring posts, no aid was sent. Moore was indignant at this conduct of his officers. Orders were then issued to destroy all the ground provisions, and to burn all the huts in the woods wherever found : he considered these measures of the greatest importance for reducing the enemy.

Thus he continued visiting every post in succession, to keep all on the alert, and attacking the enemy whenever an opportunity could be found. These assaults he generally made in person, to inspire activity and zeal; but his conduct will be understood by the following letter to his father :—

'St. Lucia, 20th August, 1796.

' My dear Father,

'I have often reproached myself with 'not writing to you; I know how anxious 'you all are about me; but since I have 'been left in this island, I have never had a 'moment I could call my own; and am at 'times so worn out, as notwithstanding my

' honours, being addressed as his Excellency,
' &c., I am infinitely more an object of pity
' than of envy.

' I received a short letter from you lately
' of the 18th June. You had then heard of
' my successful attack on the enemy, at the
' height of Chabot, and General Abercrom-
' bie's approbation of the mode in which
' that attack was conducted; but still more
' of the movement I made immediately after
' it to the heights of Chasseau. Your
' satisfaction was damped by the rumours
' which had reached you, of unsuccessful
' attacks afterwards, loss of officers, &c.
' Your letter, together with one I received
' the same day from Nesbitt, representing the
' state he had found my mother in, affected
' me so much, that I cried like a child.
' There is nothing I dread so much as your
' receiving accounts during an attack. The
' attack made upon our advanced post,
' where I commanded, the day before the sur-
' render, was more bloody than that at Chabot.
' I dreaded more than once that we should

' have been repulsed; the ground was against
' us, and we were under the grape-shot of the
' fort. Nothing but the gallantry and good
' conduct of the officers and soldiers of the
' 27th regiment saved us. The poor fellows
' when lying on the ground mangled were
' encouraging the rest; your friend Drum-
' mond cut down an officer with his sword,
' and did himself great honour. I hear he is
' so ill at Grenada as not to be expected to
' live—it is a thousand pities. Old Major
' Dunlop's son is since dead of the wound he
' received. My usual good fortune attended
' me, I escaped; and though now the sickness
' at this place is perfectly alarming, I have
' not once had a headache. Many of the
' Blacks, previous to the surrender, escaped
' with their arms into the woods and interior
' of this island. For some time they remained
' quiet, but since, encouraged by white people
' attached to the republic, and who were
' very improperly allowed to remain in
' the island, they began burning houses, and
' villages, murdering people of all ages and

' both sexes, so that it became highly neces-
' sary, not only from humanity, but for the
' safety of our posts and the colony, to march
' against them. They were joined by num-
' bers of blacks from the plantations; all of
' that colour are attached to them. I have
' not only these Brigands to subdue, but the
' coast to guard from succours which may be
' thrown in, in small boats from Guadaloupe,
' and I have unfortunately very few officers
' upon whom I can depend. The regiments
' are ill commanded, the composition of the
' inferior officers bad. Under these circum-
' stances I saw the necessity of my presence
' in every quarter. These last six weeks
' have been employed in eternal movement
' round the island; visiting the different
' posts and attacking the Brigands wherever
' I could get intelligence of their being as-
' sembled. The difficulty of this country is
' prodigious—mountains, deep and rugged
' ravines, and woods. These are extremely
' favourable to such an enemy. The coun-
' try, particularly the interior, abounds in

' ground provisions, upon which the negroes,
' who are extremely temperate, live, and are
' satisfied. It was my wish to have governed
' the colony with mildness; but I have been
' forced to adopt the most violent measures
' from the perverseness and bad composition
' of those I have to deal with. After being
' out six weeks, I returned here a few days
' ago. In that time I have undergone more
' fatigue and inconvenience, than most officers
' suffer in as many campaigns, yet it agrees
' with me, for I never was better.

   ' The Brigands are at least humbled;
' many have returned to the estates, and
' above three hundred have been killed.
' Whether I shall be able to establish tran-
' quillity I know not. I have ordered all the
' provisions on the heights to be destroyed;
' and I wish to be able to embark every black
' I take, or who surrenders. Their hatred
' to us and attachment to the Republic;
' which they think had given them liberty,
' is great. They are encouraged and sup-
' ported by white people, enemies of good

' order, and who hope to benefit by the con-
' fusion they create.

 ' What I have to fear is succours from
' Guadaloupe, of arms, ammunition, and a
' few officers. If I were obliged to withdraw
' the troops from the country and outposts,
' I should be instantly besieged in a bad post,
' where the troops are beyond conception
' unhealthy. By keeping them out, I not
' only protect the inhabitants, but preserve
' the soldiers. The inconveniences I have to
' combat are great. The representations I
' made to Sir Ralph, before his departure,
' made him angry, and I was so provoked I
' requested to be relieved from the command.
' His answer was not very gracious; but
' before his departure, perhaps he repented,
' for he wrote to me a very kind letter. I am
' now become used to difficulties. If I ex-
' tricate myself from this command with
' credit, I shall be easy the rest of my life.
' If I am besieged, do not fear the event. It
' will rather be a relief to me; everything
' will then be concentred, and I do not think

' they can take me. But this is a horrid
' war, which, together with the bad manner
' everything is conducted, the degeneracy of
' the troops, &c. &c., makes me think that
' the sooner it is over the better.

' The Journal goes on badly. The events
' are too numerous, and I have not time to
' insert them.

' I am allowed thirty shillings a-day as
' Commandant. I have not time to be ex-
' pensive, and it will ill pay every necessary
' expense. Sir Ralph wrote to me on his
' departure, that he had recommended to
' Mr. Dundas to give me a larger salary. If
' he consents, *tant mieux*, I shall in that case
' have something for a future day.

' I long to hear from you, and from Gene-
' ral Sir Charles Stuart.

*   *   *   \-

' The army we had last campaign is, or
' will be, entirely knocked up before the end
' of the hurricane weather. If Guadaloupe
' is intended to be attacked, the army must
' come from home. It is not the climate

' alone that kills the troops in this country;
' it is bad management. We seem as igno-
' rant as if we had never before made war
' in it. A Roman army would have gone
' through their military exercises in the West
' Indies and have been healthy. I differ
' from most people I meet with on this sub-
' ject; but *I am sure I am right.* As for my-
' self, I rise at daylight, go to bed at nine,
' and am during the day in eternal action. I
' have not time to be ill; I wish my mother
' and you but saw me, to be perfectly at ease
' on that score. If you wish for anything,
' wish the hurricane months over, and that
' the reputation of my activity may deter
' citoyen Victor Hughes from molesting St.
' Lucia. It may be said, how well I should
' have defended it were he to land; and that
' reputation will satisfy me. Farewell. I
' hope everybody continues well in Clifford-
' street; in their well-being is my happiness
' concentred. Ever, my dear Father, your
' affectionate son,

' J. MOORE.'

The account in the above letter represents his condition in too favourable a light, lest he should alarm his family: for the mortality among the troops had diminished their numbers so much, that he applied to Sir Ralph Abercrombie for a reinforcement. But Sir Ralph, from the same cause, refused this application; and in a manner which hurt General Moore. But some addition was quite requisite: so he repeated his request; and complained of his treatment. Sir Ralph, being then convinced of the necessity of complying with his demand, sent three hundred black troops with a kind and flattering letter, to which Moore made the following reply:

' (Private.)   Fort Charlotte, St. Lucie, 2nd Sept. 1796.

' Dear General,

   ' Your letter of the 17th July made me ' very uneasy. I was not conscious of having ' deserved, and I was extremely sorry to find, ' I had incurred your displeasure. I can ' assure you, that my exertions to fulfil the

' duties of my station were unremitting : it
' was my ambition to execute your orders,
' and to restore tranquillity to the island you
' had intrusted to my care. But from the
' little attention which I thought was paid to
' my representations, the shameful ignorance,
' and want of zeal in the principal officers
' under my command, of which fresh in-
' stances provoked me daily, made me de-
' spair of success, and was perhaps the cause
' of that impatience which appeared in my
' letters, and of which you complain. So
' many circumstances at that time combined
' to irritate and vex me, that a temper less
' warm than mine might have yielded to
' them. Had you been present, I think you
' would have been more inclined to pity than
' to be angry with me. I soon after received
' your letter of the 20th July, and I can
' never forget your attentions in writing thus
' kindly to me immediately previous to your
' departure. The arrival of Druault's corps,
' which your letter announced, was not a
' greater cordial. From that time to within

' this fortnight, I continued absent from the
' Morne. I have directed the destruction of the
' ground provisions; and taking every means
' to find out the camps and retreats of the
' Brigands, I ordered them to be attacked;
' and generally attacked them in person.
' In order to inspire some activity and zeal,
' it was necessary, I found, to show a great
' deal. The Brigands, from being extremely
' insolent, frequently approaching, and even
' attacking our posts, soon became less enter-
' prising. They have had, upon the whole,
' I suppose, between three and four hundred
' people killed, wounded, and hanged; and
' are, from every report, much disheartened.
' Many have returned upon the estates, driven
' by fear and hunger, but still equally disaf-
' fected. The greater number, however, con-
' tinue in the woods, and are encouraged to
' bear with every inconvenience, from the
' hopes of being soon succoured from Gua-
' daloupe.

    ' Many have lately had communication
' with that island. I do what I can to guard

' the coast with troops, but it is too extensive,
' and too rugged to be guarded effectually
' by other means than shipping. Every
' representation has been made to the Ad-
' miral, but hitherto the windward coast has
' been completely open. The Brigands have
' been so driven, and must be so much dis-
' tressed for provisions, that I am convinced,
' could all communication be intercepted for
' three weeks, the business would be over,
' and tranquillity restored to the island; but
' any succours from Guadaloupe will throw
' everything back, and may be attended with
' serious consequences, from the dispersed
' and sickly condition of the troops.

' I have lately arrested many individuals
' who had remained in consequence of the
' terms of the capitulation, and of the first
' proclamation. There was every reason to
' suspect them of having assisted the Brigands
' with provisions, ammunition, and intelli-
' gence. I have been forced to adopt other
' violent measures, which at first I had flat-
' tered myself would not have been necessary;

' but true republicanism seems, at least in
' this country, to be an excuse for every
' species of treachery, want of faith, and even
' of common honesty ; and I begin to think
' that harsh measures, to which the republic
' has accustomed them, can alone be effi-
' cacious. Whether I shall succeed or not
' in finally restoring tranquillity, I cannot
' say ; it depends so much on accident and
' the efforts of others.

' As far as my abilities go, I have, and
' shall continue to exert them. I have under-
' gone a degree of personal inconvenience
' and fatigue, which circumstances rendered
' necessary, but which few constitutions are
' equal to ; mine has hitherto resisted, and
' I am perfectly well. I wish I could say as
' much for the officers and men under my
' command. These have suffered severely.
' The sickness is so much greater upon
' Morne Fortuné and its immediate depen-
' dencies, than at the other posts, that I de-
' tain upon it a number only sufficient for the
' daily duties. The troops, I observe, which

' have been most active, are the most healthy,
' a proof that the sun is not the cause of the
' sickness.   There are local situations in
' these islands (Morne Fortuné is unfortu-
' nately one of them) which are so unhealthy,
' that perhaps no care or management could
' totally counteract.   But in general, the
' greater part of the sickness proceeds from
' the want of interior discipline and economy
' in the regiments.

' Great attention should be paid in this
' country to the cleanliness, and even neat-
' ness of the soldier's person, and the regu-
' larity of his diet; an addition to the eating
' part of the ration, instead of rum; sea, or
' river bathing, constant activity, and move-
' ment.   In short, General, (excuse the
' pedantry of the expression,) but with a
' Roman, instead of modern exercise and
' discipline, the troops in the West Indies
' might, I am convinced, be kept healthy.
' A parade twice a day, consisting of a mere
' inspection and exercise of arms, is easy for
' officers; it leaves them what they call more

' time: but it leaves the soldier also to
' lounge the whole day in a barrack, where
' the air cannot be good; and where, from
' indolence, his body becomes enervated and
' liable to disorder.

' The army you left in this country is
' almost entirely melted away. The officers
' and men are dispirited; the former thinking
' only of getting home, and framing excuses,
' in many instances the most shameful, to
' bring it about.

' I fear the same fate (should the war con-
' tinue) will attend whatever troops are sent
' out, unless serious attention is paid to get
' proper officers to put at the head of regi-
' ments, who will re-establish discipline, and
' inspire those under them with some of that
' zeal and ardour, which I am not too young
' to have seen, but which you must recollect
' so much better to have existed in the
' service. Such officers, I am sure, still exist
' in the British army, though they are not to
' be found exclusively amongst those who
' have most money, or most political interest.

' In th's country, much may be made of
' black corps. I have had occasion to observe
' them of late. They possess, I think, many
' excellent qualities as soldiers, and may,
' with proper attention, become equal to any
' thing; even at present, as they are, for the
' West Indies they are invaluable.

' I ought to apologise to you for this long
' discursion, into which I have been led in-
' sensibly. What I have observed of the
' state of the army since I came to the West
' Indies has made an impression upon me,
' and I much fear, if strong remedies are not
' applied, that the British army will lose
' even that character for spirit which has
' hitherto distinguished it.

' I write to you with a degree of freedom
' to which I am not entitled, but which I
' hope you will excuse.

' We have had no intelligence from
' England this long time, the 18th or 19th
' June are the latest.

' I have the honour to be, &c. &c. &c.,

JOHN MOORE.'

' His Excellency Sir R. Abercrombie.'

Soon after writing the above, intelligence was received that supplies from Guadaloupe, for the Brigands, had been landed on the coast. Moore immediately set off for Vieux-Fort, and as it was unsafe to go by land without a strong escort, he went in a six-oared canoe, with Brigade-Major Anderson. After proceeding some leagues, the coxswain, a sharp-sighted negro, saw a canoe, a great way a-head, advancing from the shore, and bending towards them. This excited surprise, as strict orders had been issued to destroy every kind of boat; and assurances were returned, that those orders had been punctually executed. One of the rowers next saw another canoe pursuing from behind, which rendered it impossible to return. The negroes in the boat were terrified; they had no arms on board, and well knew, that if the fell savages overtook them, they would murder them all and cast their bodies into the sea. The coxswain, who possessed some intelligence, signified to Moore, that he could neither proceed nor attempt to return to St. Lucia, without being overtaken with certainty;

and that the next island, though out of sight,
was St. Vincent.   Moore then said, ' To that
' shore direct your course.'   They immediately
put out to sea, and the negro rowers plied their
oars with all their might.   The chase continued
till near sunset, when the coxswain, whose
eyes were fixed on the pursuers, observed that
they had slackened their speed ; and soon
afterwards he gave the glad tidings that they
were returning to the shore.   The negroes,
almost exhausted and breathless, then rested
on their oars.   After it became dark, the
original course was resumed, and by taking
a wide circuitous sweep, and rowing all night,
they reached Vieux-Fort safely in the morning. It was learnt afterwards that a spy at
the Morne had transmitted intelligence, and
that this was a premeditated plot to intercept
the Governor.

On his arrival, he visited all the posts,
searched for the camps of the Brigands, and
sent out detachments in various directions,
to assail and harass them.   Although his
constitution was excellent, the fatigue he

suffered, together with the burning heat of
the sun, threw him into the baneful fever of
the climate. It was a disease from which
few recovered: but, after lying three weeks in
a most dangerous state, the fever remitted,
and he was moved to Fort Charlotte*, by sea.
There he relapsed, and was for a week in
most imminent danger; when unexpectedly
he got the better of this second attack also,
although he was reduced to a very weak condition. During this illness he received letters from General Hunter, who commanded at
St. Vincent, stating that Marin Padre, the
Commander of the Charibs and Brigands of
St. Vincent, had surrendered upon terms:
he had brought in most of his men, and
peace was nearly restored to that island.
This mulatto, Marin Padre, was a small pro-
prietor of St. Lucia, and had great influence
with the blacks there. Moore, therefore,
wrote to General Hunter, that if Marin would
undertake and succeed in inducing the Brigands here to surrender, all his property

The Citadel at the Morne.

should be restored to him. This man readily accepted the proposition, and General Hunter testified, that in several negotiations, he had acted with good faith, and that his character was noted for honesty and humanity.

Marin Padre was then sent over to Fort Charlotte, and when questioned by Moore, answered with great apparent ingenuity: he said he should be most happy if he could persuade the Brigands to surrender upon the same terms as those in St. Vincent, and he thought they would, if the Governor would promise to pardon them. He added, that, for his own part, he wished of all things to see tranquillity restored to the island, where all his relatives were.

The Brigands having lately received considerable supplies, Moore considered that moment unfavourable for negotiating: but after defeating them repeatedly in several encounters, and discovering and destroying their deposits of ammunition, Marin Padre was despatched to try what could be done by a negotiation. In a few days a letter was sent in, signed by La Croix, Commandant l'Armée Françoise dans les bois, who offered to treat, but wished to know on what terms. It was answered, that he and the armed men should be considered as prisoners of war; and that the negroes who had quitted the estates must return to them, and should be treated with humanity. He asked for a month to assemble and consult his people, and during that time hostilities should cease. Instead of a month, forty-eight hours were granted.

He then wrote that he would consult the chiefs, and in eight days send an answer; none, however, came. Yet Marin Padre, who had seen La Croix frequently, assured the Governor that he was in earnest in wishing the negroes to surrender. The term, however, elapsed without any answer being transmitted: when a young emigrant officer, trusting to the truce, imprudently went into the woods to shoot; and fell in with some Brigands, who murdered him. Marin Padre declared that this frightened La Croix, who dreaded retaliation, and had prevented his approaching our posts to communicate; so he was sent again in search of him. But no further communication being made, Moore suspected that La Croix only intended to gain time, or put him off his guard. He, therefore, recommenced hostilities with vigour; and while he was thus hotly engaged, a vessel arrived from Martinico, with a letter from the Commander-in-Chief, who wished to see him immediately.

He went aboard a vessel on the 10th of January, 1797, and had the pleasure of joining his friends, Sir Ralph Abercrombie and General Hope, the same evening. Sir Ralph then expressed great regret at his having been so long detained at a post of such extreme anxiety and fatigue as St. Lucia; that it was only just he should be relieved, though he owned he knew not whom to send in his place. He then signified that the government of Grenada was vacant, which Moore might have if he pleased; or, as it was intended to join the Barrack Department to the Quarter-Master General's office, which would be permanent, even in peace, he might have that lucrative appointment if he preferred it. Moore replied,* 'that his greatest 'wish was to be useful to him and to his 'country; that the island of St. Lucia might 'still be lost, if not closely attended to; and 'as he was now thoroughly acquainted with 'the country, perhaps he was more fit to 'preserve it than any one he could at present 'find. He did not court money, and was 'satisfied with his approbation; but were 'any active military operations to be under-'taken, he should certainly wish to be em-'ployed with him, otherwise he was content 'to remain at St. Lucia.'

That very night he received letters, stating that the post of Prasline had been surprised by the Brigands; the commanding officer, and most of the men, killed, and consternation spread over the whole country.

Moore communicated this intelligence to

* Journal, MS.

Sir Ralph, and sailed back immediately to his government. On his arrival, he learned that the officer commanding at Prasline had become negligent; that his men were almost all bathing in a river, and he himself asleep, when the Brigands set upon them. He then roused himself, got a few men under arms, but most of them were frightened, and ran off, as is apt to happen in unexpected alarms. The Commander himself fought courageously, and received two wounds. But perceiving that his men would give way, and being resolved not to survive the disgrace incurred, he drew out a pistol and shot himself.

The quick return of their Governor diffused spirits among the disheartened troops, and restored confidence to the island. Vessels, which were seen watching opportunities to land more supplies to the army, were prevented by increased vigilance. Prasline was re-occupied, a detachment surprised the Brigand camp, killed some, dispersed the rest, and regained the provisions which had been captured.

Other corps were sent out in various directions to scour the woods, and to root up every
esculent vegetable.

When Moore was hastening with a small
escort from the post of Gros-Ilet to Marquis,
an express brought him intelligence that Denerie, distant six hours' march, was attacked
by a horde of Brigands. A small corps from
Marquis was moving to reinforce that post;
and Moore's escort being over-fatigued,
he took twenty of the freshest men of the
other corps, with whom he pushed on to
Denerie. He arrived near that post at nine
at night; deep silence prevailed, and several
houses were on fire. As it was prudent to
ascertain first in whose possession the post
then was, he took precautions, and advanced
cautiously in the dark. The ground in front
of the palisades was strewed with the bodies
of dead negroes; and British sentinels were
seen behind the parapet. When he entered,
Lieutenant Le Brun received him exultingly,
happy at having sustained, with only fifty
men, the furious assaults of above three hun-

dred Brigands for three hours. He had not
only repulsed them, but sallied out and pursued them into the woods, with considerable
slaughter.

Moore bestowed deserved encomiums oh
this gallant youth, a French emigrant, and on
his brave garrison.

About a year after this, my brother introduced me to the above officer, who had returned from St. Lucia in bad health. He
was wan, pale, and dejected: but my brother,
by urgent recommendations at the Horse-
Guards, obtained for him a company in a
foreign corps, which highly gratified him.

While Moore was engaged in the per-
plexed affairs of St. Lucia, Sir Ralph Abercrombie proceeded against Trinidad, and
afterwards against Porto Rico : and he apo-
logized to Moore for still leaving him behind,
declaring that he knew not by whom to
replace him. Notwithstanding which, it was
a mortification to Moore not to share in important enterprises ; and he was also apprehensive lest the enemy should take advantage

of the absence of the principal fleet and army
to land supplies. He took every precaution
in his power to hinder this, by guarding well
the coast; and his detachments defeated the
Brigands in many skirmishes, and harassed
them with inroads on all sides. By these
unceasing operations, and by famine, their
obdurate tempers began to yield, and numbers surrendered: and some of the few who
remained in the woods were daily coming
in to submit; so Moore had the certain prospect of soon restoring tranquillity to that
unhappy island. But during this time the
troops were sinking by disease; and his own
constitution proved incapable of sustaining
the exertions he made. He rose usually at
six in the morning, was occupied in business
till mid-day; then marched frequently in
that sultry clime thirty miles a-day, and slept
in his clothes on the ground. He was thus
in continual exercise, until again seized with
the yellow fever; and was well acquainted
with the usual fatality of secondary attacks of that malignant distemper. Indeed,

though young, he had witnessed all the various ghastly forms of death, and concluded
that his own mortal career was now about to
close. The malady being infectious, he was
shunned by all, except by his faithful friend
Anderson, and a trusty servant. Every
remedy failed ; he sunk into a state of insen-
sibility, and in this last extremity, his medical attendant not being at hand, Anderson
went in search of another physician, who
refused to visit the Governor, when his case
was hopeless, on the plea that he ought to
have been sent for sooner.

Anderson returned, and from the appear-
ances doubted whether his friend had not
breathed his last. But finding some warmth
in the body, he poured down a little wine, and·
continued administering more and more, from
observing that the breathing became percep-
tible, and that animation seemed to revive.
The Attendant-Surgeon then came in, who
was astonished at finding him still alive. Wine
and other remedies were persisted in ; the
fever ceased, and an unexpected amendment

ensued.. When lying in the last extremity, a report was carried to Martinico that he had died, and Colonel Drummond arrived to take the command. He found the Governor somewhat better; but only enabled to give verbal instructions, and quite incapable of acting. He was lifted from his bed, carried aboard a vessel, and transported to Martinico. There he communicated with Sir Ralph Abercrombie, and pointed out the measures requisite to complete the reduction of St. Lucia ; which plan was followed, and soon proved successful. Sir Ralph, on witnessing Moore's feeble and declining health, recommended his immediate return to England. Thus his toils in St. Lucia terminated, and with success. But fame is only won on great occasions, as by that memorable battle, when an oft-victorious Emperor was chased from the field and dethroned. Whereas, in a petty warfare for an inconsiderable island, whatever military skill may be exerted, whatever difficulties surmounted, or perils from a barbarous enemy and pestilential clime encountered, they remain unknown or unheeded.

In sailing homewards, the fresh sea-breezes renovated Moore's strength, and exhilarated his spirits. He landed at Falmouth, and reached his father's house, in London, in July ; when his sallow looks and emaciated form were sad indications of the dangers he had passed.

MOORE's return to his paternal home spread joy among his parents, his sister, and brothers; and as happiness is as salutary, as misery is deleterious, by sharing their feelings, his eyes brightened, his colour cleared, and his strength was restored. Yet little leisure was allowed him for domestic pleasures, for tranquillity and ambition are incompatible. Whenever, by promoting the public-weal, distinction is aimed at, ease must be relinquished, toil embraced, and anxiety endured.

Moore was received by the Duke of York with a friendly welcome, and Mr. Secretary Dundas made particular inquiries respecting St. Lucia, requesting from him a detailed opinion in writing of the value, and of the force requisite for the defence of the island.

A memorial was accordingly drawn up and delivered to that minister.

As an invasion from France was then seriously apprehended, Major Hay, of the Engineers, was directed to make a survey of the eastern coast of England, and Moore accompanied him on that duty. Every part, where a landing by the enemy could be effected, was carefully examined, and a full report was given in by the Major.

Hitherto Moore had served against his country's foreign enemies, but it now became his lot to be called out to act against intestine foes. For soon after the beginning of the war with France, some perfidious Irishmen had commenced a secret correspondence with the French Government, and had urged the invasion of their country. To favour a descent, secret societies, bound together by treasonable oaths, were organized; and assurances were transmitted to France, that whenever an army should land, multitudes of the Irish Catholics would join them.

France was then ruled by the depraved

Directory : whose government the misguided Irish were taught to believe was preferable to the British, and that the presence of a French army in the heart of their country was desirable.

To take advantage of this infatuation, and, by the aid of traitors, to conquer Ireland, a fleet and army were assembled at Brest. Secrecy was so well observed, that neither the time, nor the place for the disembarkation, was communicated even to the conspirators. But the depth of winter was fixed upon for the attempt, to have the better chance of escaping from the British fleet.

On the 10th of December, 1796, transports containing twenty-five thousand soldiers, escorted by eighteen ships of the line and thirteen frigates, sailed from Brest. The British Admiral lying at Spithead received intelligence of their departure, but learnt nothing of the course they had taken. He steered his course towards Brest, and missed the French fleet, which encountered a storm, and was much dispersed.

. The frigate, on board of which Hoche the commander had embarked, was blown far to the westward; while the other ships reached in succession Bantry Bay, in the south of Ireland. But no one, in the absence of the Commander, had instructions what to do. So after a short stay the French fleet sailed back to Brest, losing two ships of the line, and several frigates and transports, which foundered at sea, or were captured.

The project, though thus frustrated, was not abandoned; and the Irish malcontents, convinced by the attempt, that the French were in earnest in offering them assistance, became more turbulent and outrageous than before. Upon which reinforcements of troops were sent over to Ireland; and the militia and the well-affected were arrayed. As the loyal inhabitants were in general Protestants, and the disaffected Catholics, religion was on this occasion, as on others, made a pretext for taking up arms. The divine doctrine, to love our neighbours as ourselves, was reversed; hatred inculcated, and political enmity was exasperated by religious rancour. In the collision of these furious passions, many atrocities were committed by the Irish on each other; and when the military were called in to restore peace, they were always insulted, and frequently opposed. Provocations excited retaliation, and the soldiers also became guilty of illegal acts. Such was the dismal state of Ireland, when a second hostile expedition was fitted out at the urgent instigation of the Irish rebels. This armament was secretly assembled in Holland, and a fleet of Dutch men of war sailed from the Texel in October, 1797. Admiral Duncan, who commanded on that station, proceeded vigilantly in quest of the enemy. He descried, overtook, and discomfited the Dutch fleet: one half of which was captured, and the rest escaped in a shattered condition.

This defeat rendered all immediate succours from France very doubtful; yet it did not discourage the disaffected Irish from their determination of breaking out into insurrection. The plot was communicated to government, and the chief command of the army given to Sir Ralph Abercrombie, who applied for Moore to be appointed Brigadier-General under him. This was immediately acceded to, and both reached Dublin on the 2nd of December.

Previous to this, the military force had been scattered over the country in separate detachments to assist the civil power. This dispersion gave the agitators an opportunity of debauching the soldiers; many of whom were tempted to take oaths contrary to their allegiance, discontents were fomented against their officers, and discipline and subordination were impaired. The Commander-in-Chief, resolving to correct immediately the disorders in the army, began by collecting the troops into large bodies. He then issued an order, in which the Generals and Commanding Officers of corps were enjoined to pay strict attention to their duty, to correct the licentious state of the troops, and to restore order and obedience.

As the generals of districts, and commanders of Irish corps, had been accustomed
to be complimented, they could not bear the
truth.   They first murmured, and then declaimed against this order, which surrep-
titiously got into the public newspapers.   It
was there virulently commented upon with
factious malignity, as a libel upon our brave
army, whose conduct, it was asserted, merited
the highest praise.   And the opponents to
government artfully quoted it, as a complete
proof, or indeed, an acknowledgment, that
the riots and disaffection which had prevailed,
were solely owing to the misconduct of the
soldiers.   One sentence was particularly
dwelt upon, in which the General enjoined,
' that the military should not act, except in
' the presence, and by the authority of a
' Civil Magistrate.'   This injunction was
noticed as contradictory to a proclamation
from the Lord Lieutenant, issued before Sir
Ralph had the command.   Sir Ralph had
not been aware of that proclamation, and
having newly arrived in the country, con-

ceived that the tumults and irregularities
might be suppressed by lenient means. The
ferment against him at last rose so high,
that apprehensions of a serious nature began to be entertained. On which a fresh proclamation, similar to the first, and a correspondent order were issued; and Sir Ralph
Abercrombie, who was devoid of political
circumspection, judged it prudent to resign
the command, which was conferred on
General Lake.

But before his resignation, he visited, along
with Brigadier Moore, the southern coast,
where an invasion was chiefly apprehended.
The harbour of Cork, Bantry Bay, and
the fortifications along the adjacent shores,
were all examined; and the defensive preparations were found in a very defective state.
They were also not a little surprised to find
a volunteer corps clothed in the French uniform. The commanding officer was sharply
reprimanded, who alleged in his defence, that
he knew not that it was the French dress.

The chief command of this district was

given to Sir James Stewart, who was in a
bad state of health, and resided in the city
of Cork. Moore fixed his quarters at Bandon. The troops under his immediate command exceeded three thousand, and were
considered the advanced southern corps of the
army. They chiefly consisted of Irish militia; the officers were Protestants, and most
of the men Catholics, who bore ill will to their
officers, and were exceedingly disaffected.
To check the irregularities of those men of
lawless habits, and to form them to obedience, was a difficult task. But notwithstanding their faults, they were a fine body of
soldiers, and remarkably good tempered; so
by kind, yet strict management, Moore
gradually brought them into tolerable order.
Among other regulations, he never suffered
the bands to play tunes grating to Irish
feelings; and to prevent the jarring of the
discordant parties, the soldiers were marched
to church without music. Severity was very
rarely had recourse to, but could not always,
with these unruly men, be dispensed with.

Once a plot of a dangerous kind. was detected in a militia regiment. On its discovery, three men deserted, and eight or nine were arrested. They were tried, punished, and sent abroad.

Anonymous letters of complaint from another regiment were received, on which Moore addressed the men on the parade. He spoke to them mildly yet authoritatively: and told them, that if they thought themselves aggrieved, they had a right, by the articles of war, to state their grievances openly to him. This was accordingly done: when it was found that there were, in fact, some grounds for the discontents; and these were consequently redressed. He also frequently received reports, both publicly and privately, of conspiracies and intended risings of the people; and accusations were made of individuals against each other, which were sometimes true, and at other times false. Patriotism prompted the first, party zeal, mingled with the most malignant animosity, stimulated the latter. A younger brother of a good family informed against his elder, who possessed a considerable estate, that he had secreted a great quantity of arms in his garden. All the premises were carefully searched, but no arms were found. This instance of fraternal treachery reminded Moore of the Roman proscriptions, when kindred affections, and all moral principles, were extinguished.

As in various parts of the country tumultuous meetings, training to arms, and assassinations of public functionaries augmented, government, in the month of April, proclaimed that rebellion had broken out, and orders were sent to Moore to disarm the inhabitants near the coast. He proceeded himself to the most disaffected part, with five companies of light infantry, and a party of dragoons, and sent another detachment in another direction. But instead of suffering the soldiers to live at large, the parishes were summoned to bring in the exact rations requisite, and no waste was made. Strict discipline was observed ; and the soldiers were not allowed to wander from their posts; which hindered them from plundering, or injuring the people. Notice was then promulgated to the inhabitants to bring in arms of every kind. The people were at first stubborn, and denied that they had any; but after four days a number were given up. Moore then proceeded to other places, and exhorted the inhabitants to deliver up their arms, as otherwise he should be forced to permit the troops to live at free quarters. These measures occasioned great terror. But the troops were immediately removed from those parishes which obeyed. He thus fulfilled his orders with as little violence as possible, and collected three or four hundred firelocks, and about eight hundred pikes.

The Protestant landholders, who had been in serious alarm, were much pleased with the disarming; but instead of attachment, great animosity subsisted between them and their Catholic tenantry and peasantry. Moore counselled them strongly to moderate their resentment, and to endeavour to acquire

the good will of the people, for otherwise
the pikes would soon re-appear. The prudence and humanity of his treatment of
the Irish was censured by some hot spirits,
who called aloud for vengeance, yet it proved
successful by being accompanied with unceasing watchfulness. Wherever assemblies
were intended, or risings threatened, he
either suddenly appeared there, or sent a
strong detachment of cavalry and infantry,
which overawed the malcontents; by which
conduct, though his district was considered
to be the most disaffected of any, no insurrection broke out in it.

Certainly, the brute creation, who are
merely guided by instinct, never act so
preposterously, as the rational frequently
do.   For it appears from history, that
nations at certain periods became frantic, and
brought misery upon themselves. The poets
explain this by inventing the allegory of the
Furies armed with snakes and torches, bursting out of hell, and instilling madness into
the people. But in plain truth these Furies

are wicked and ambitious men; skilled in the art of deceiving the populace, and of inflaming their passions, in order to obtain for themselves wealth, power, or fame. This was now strikingly exemplified in Ireland; in which island, agriculture, commerce, and manufactures were more prosperous, than in any former age; and the arts, sciences, and civilization, were also progressively advancing. But instead of allowing this amelioration to proceed, the nation was instigated to open rebellion; by which all improvement retrograded, and the people were involved in misery. As traitors fortunately are rarely trusty to each other, certain information of the plot was conveyed to government a few weeks before the revolt broke out. Several of the conspirators were instantly seized and cast into prison; and it is painful to relate that there was one man of quality, who, forgetful of his high birth and station, was fired with the mad ambition of being a chief of rebels.

When his accomplices were arrested he concealed himself; but his lurking place was discovered; and in resisting the police officers he was shot, and thus escaped dying on a scaffold.

When these transactions were taking place at Dublin, Moore remained at Bandon and the neighbourhood, watching events. No mail arrived on the 26th of May, nor on the subsequent days, but abundant reports were brought in by some persons evidently frightened, and by others secretly glad, that Dublin and the whole surrounding country had risen in arms. On the 28th, a letter was delivered to Moore, from Sir James Stewart, to desire that he would come immediately to Cork, which it was feared would break out in insurrection. He went there and stayed two days, and measures of prevention were adopted. He then returned to preserve tranquillity at his own post at Bandon; and as this was the moment when an invasion from France was to be expected, the troops were kept on the alert, and orders were sent to all the outposts on the coast to be vigilant.

After some days of anxious expectation, accounts from Dublin were brought by sea; the land communication being interrupted. It appeared that the arrest of Lord Edward Fitzgerald, and other leaders of the rebels, had disconcerted their plans; and the revolt was neither general nor well-conducted. It was at Kildare, in the vicinity of Dublin, and in the King and Queen's County, that the infuriated peasantry first rose up. Some were armed with fowling-pieces, others with muskets privately conveyed from France, and many with long pikes secretly fabricated at home, which in determined hands are formidable weapons.

On the 23d of May, multitudes of these wild men, congregated into bands, under ferocious chiefs, burst simultaneously in the middle of the night into several towns in Kildare. At Claire* and Neis, the Com-

* History of the Rebellion in Ireland, 1798, by the Rev. James Gordon.

mandants being vigilant, the assailants were
repulsed. But the rebels stole into the little
town of Prosperous unperceived. Some soldiers were savagely murdered in their quarters; the barrack was set on fire, and twenty-
eight militiamen with their Captain were
consumed by the flames, or stabbed with
pikes in attempting to escape. Two days
after this, a dreadful retaliation was perpetrated by their countrymen at the town of
Carlow; for a column of rebels who had
assaulted that place, being put to flight, some
of the fugitives took shelter in the houses,
which were immediately set fire to. Several
other towns were also attempted; but fire-
arms and discipline prevailed over brutal
fury. As a considerable body of troops were
prudently quartered in Dublin, where ammunition and stores had been accumulated, that
city was prevented from revolting, which
gave the opportunity of sending forth detachments against the insurgents elsewhere,
before their leaders could reduce them to
order. They were consequently defeated in

several small encounters, and great numbers of these misguided men were miserably
slain. The remainder, being quite disheartened, dispersed; and that part of the country
was tranquillized. But affairs wore a far
more menacing appearance in Wicklow and
Wexford: for in these counties very few
troops were stationed, as the inhabitants were
less suspected. But they also flew to arms
in great bodies, and cut off several small
parties, who moved against them without
concert. Even two small detachments, which
were pushed on from Duncannon Fort, by
General Fawcet, were surrounded and massacred. By these successes the rebels acquired arms, and two pieces of cannon; and
were so greatly encouraged, that they drove
out the garrisons from Wexford and Enniscorthy, and ravaged the adjoining country.
Wherever the insurgents reached, they
burned and plundered farms and dwelling-
houses, sparing neither age nor sex. For in
this advanced age of the world, during the
French Revolution and the Irish Rebellion,

hostilities were not confined to those bearing arms. Even peaceful persons were often dragged from their domestic homes, and cruelly massacred; while the ruthless murderers derided the wailings and agonies of their dying victims.

These horrible consequences ought to induce statesmen vigilantly to prevent, or extinguish, the first sparks of civil commotion: for, unhappily, there are sullen, malignant spirits ever at work, to kindle discontents among the people, and, when the fire has caught, to fan the flame.

The number of the insurgents continuing to augment, they were emboldened to attempt the conquest of New Ross, a considerable town garrisoned with twelve hundred regular troops, commanded by General Johnstone. It was projected by the rebels to attack the town on three sides at once; but this plan was ill-executed by these disorderly men. One dense mass, however, rushed into the heart of the town, with levelled pikes, driving before them the soldiers who were posted to oppose them. But Johnstone rallied the troops with military skill; he planted cannon in proper places, and when the rebels were thrown into confusion by the fire, he ordered a charge, and pushed them out of the town. The rebels, being very numerous, were not dismayed, but exasperated by this repulse: they renewed the contest, and made several desperate assaults; yet they were finally discomfited, with the loss of nearly two thousand men.

Another great body of insurgents received a sanguinary defeat at Arklow; after which they adopted defensive measures. They retained possession of Wexford and Enniscorthy, and formed a large camp on Vinegar Hill, as their strong hold, where they commenced training; and great numbers poured in from the surrounding country to join them.

The vicissitudes which had occurred, and the accumulating strength of the rebels, prompted General Lake to assemble all his dis-

posable troops before he marched against
them. Besides calling in other detachments,
he sent for Brigadier Moore, who was lying
at Bandon, near two hundred miles distant
from Dublin. On receiving his orders, he
hastened, with a small corps of light troops,
to Cork, where Sir James Stewart commanded; but alarms of a rising in that
neighbourhood induced Sir James to detain
Moore three days. At length, in consequence
of peremptory orders, he was allowed to proceed. By rapid marches, he arrived, in a
week, at New Ross, when General Johnstone
resolved, with this reinforcement, to attack,
next day, the enemy's posts, who were assembled on Carrickburn mountain, close to the
town. The insurgents were drawn up on
heights, and in several actions had boldly
encountered the regular troops.

The British advanced early in the morning
to attack them; Johnstone led the central
column, and Moore advanced with the light
troops towards the left : but on coming within
cannon-shot, the rebels drew off: they were

pursued, and about seventy of them were shot by Moore's riflemen. General Johnstone then returned to New Ross, and directed Moore, with six field-pieces, and a thousand light troops, to proceed on the road to Wexford, to a place called Fook's Mill, where he would be joined by two regiments, commanded by Lord Dalhousie, newly landed from England; and with this reinforcement march to Taghmon, seven miles from Wexford, where he would receive fresh instructions.

His march was through a fertile and beautiful country, yet entirely deserted by the inhabitants, and many of the houses were in flames. The spectacle was mournful. On the 20th of June, Moore encamped in a gentleman's park, near Fook's Mill, and sent out parties to patrole for several miles, on all sides, to obtain intelligence of the enemy, and of the regiments that were to join him. No information was procured; but as it was in General Johnstone's plan, that Moore should that day reach Taghmon, he resolved, lest any disappointment should ensue, to set off for that place, without waiting longer for Lord Dalhousie. He began his march in the evening, but had not proceeded far, when he descried a cloud of dust blown towards him, and soon discovered that this was raised by an army of rebels advancing in his front. He had before reconnoitred the ground, and knowing it well, made his disposition accordingly.

He pushed forward some Yager riflemen to commence skirmishing; then planted his field-pieces on a commanding eminence, and drew up his light troops in the fields on both sides of the road.

The enemy amounted to between five and six thousand men, partly armed with fire-locks, but the greater number with long pikes. They rushed impetuously on his right flank, in spite of the cannonade; and the soldiers, who had never been engaged before, hesitated. Seeing this, Moore dismounted, leaped over a high ditch on the right side of the road, and putting himself at the head of the line, charged, and drove the enemy down a hill and over a bridge in their rear.

While thus engaged, his troops on the left were furiously attacked by another strong mass of the rebels. He sent a reinforcement, with a field-piece, in that direction, being unwilling to leave his post, as the enemy threatened to repass the bridge. But mes-senger after messenger came for more aid, and the fire on the left became hotter and hotter. He sent Major Anderson to learn the true state of things, who quickly reported that his presence and a reinforcement on the left were absolutely necessary. He galloped towards the spot, and found the Yagers, the infantry, and dragoons, all mingled together, falling back in confusion along the road, and the enemy pursuing them closely. He rallied his soldiers, and made some quit the road to form a front on each side of it. By his ex-hortations order was in some degree restored, and they fired briskly. When they appeared emboldened, he rode forward, commanded them to charge, and the rebels were instantaneously routed. Many fell by the bayonet, and the rest were chased from the field. They made some ineffectual attempts to collect, and make a stand; but were hotly pursued until they dispersed.

Towards the conclusion of the action news arrived of the approach of Lord Dalhousie, who, hearing the firing, had hastened on, but was too late to share in the victory; which was gained, not without the loss of several gallant officers, and a number of brave men.

As the day was far spent, and the soldiers much fatigued, Moore allowed them to rest; and they lay that night on the field of battle. Early next morning he proceeded to Taghmon; adopting on the march the necessary precautions against any surprise.

The country was totally abandoned: the houses had been burnt or plundered by the rebels, and furniture, pictures and libraries were destroyed, or strewed on the ground. At length a few pikemen, bearing a flag of truce, were seen approaching to meet the ad-

vanced guard. Major Anderson, who commanded, ordered them to halt, and send
forward an officer, whom he saw in a red
uniform. This person proved to be Lord
Kingsborough, who had unfortunately been
captured. He presented a letter from Keough,
who had assumed the title of Governor of
Wexford. It contained a proposal, that the
garrison should deliver up the town of Wexford, and lay down their arms, on condition
of a general pardon being granted, and their
property being secured to them.

Moore returned for answer, that he had no
authority to treat; and Lord Kingsborough,
having given his parole, was necessitated to
return with the pikemen.

By this means, and by the arrival of a
troop of Irish yeomanry, the miserable condition of Wexford was learnt; on which
Moore judged it expedient to push on directly
to the relief of that town, instead of marching, according to his orders, to Taghmon.

On the way he got upon a high dyke, with
two of his aide-de-camps, to examine the
country; when he saw five or six stout fel-

lows with long pikes lurking behind. A fiery young officer drew his sword, leaped down among them, and was stabbed in the arm with a pike: the Irishmen ran off and escaped, the General not permitting the soldiers to fire at them.

When he came in view of Wexford, and was winding his march along the side of the mountain called the Forth, he saw by his eye-glass, on its summit, a multitude of armed men. He detached forward a strong advanced guard to gain possession of the top of the mountain, and to hold it until the main column, together with the artillery and baggage, had all passed along the low road securely.

The rebels, on seeing the approach of the detachment, abandoned the heights, ran headlong down the hill, and through the town. Such was the terror inspired by the late defeat. And as one house was already in flames, Moore was apprehensive of the town being burnt, or of some horrid outrages being perpetrated. The yeomanry, alarmed for the safety of their relatives, drew their swords and galloped on; and Moore sent forward Lord Dalhousie with a body of troops to release all the prisoners, and to preserve the town and the inhabitants. He followed himself, as soon as he had posted his forces properly, and beheld a scene of a most affecting nature.

The prison-doors had been thrown open, and in the streets were seen wives with clamorous transport embracing their husbands, or fainting in their arms; and children screaming and clinging with their little hands to their fathers' necks, who had been doomed to death. While others, who had discovered the certain fate of their dearest relatives, were bewailing their loss with bitter tears. For on the day before, seventy prisoners had been hauled forth from their dungeons to the bridge, stabbed with pikes; and the dead bodies stripped naked and cast into the river. The merciless rebels had determined to execute all the other prisoners on that very day; who amounted to some hundreds; many of them were persons of the first rank and respectability in the country. Moore had, therefore, the singular good fortune, by exceeding his orders and hastening to Wexford, to rescue from a miserable death these innocent persons, who hailed him as their preserver.* Could the bulk of mankind profit by history, surely the preachers of the benign doctrines of Christ, and lay-political agitators, would curb their zeal and ambition, and cease to stir up and inflame the ignorant multitude, with the pretexts of religion and liberty. For experience has often evinced the horrible events which thence ensue; together with an augmentation of impiety, immorality, and the loss of rational freedom.

The operations of the principal army under the Commander-in-chief were also crowned with success. He formed a junction with General Johnstone, and stormed the rebel

---

* This conduct of General Moore was duly appreciated by the Commander-in-chief, who stated in his despatches, ' That General ' Moore, with his usual enterprise and activity, pushed on to this ' town (Wexford), and entered it so opportunely, as to prevent it ' from being laid in ashes, and the massacre of the remaining pri- ' soners, which the rebels declared their resolution of carrying into ' effect the next day.'—*London Gazette Extraordinary*, June 26, 1798.

camp on Vinegar-Hill, destroying great numbers of the enemy, and putting the rest to flight.

These victorious troops all assembled at Wexford, and the three Generals dined to- gether. To complete Moore's satisfaction at the felicitous service he had performed, his brother Graham, who commanded a fine frigate, cruising on the coast to intercept succours from France, came ashore to meet him. This delightful meeting of the brothers did not exceed half an hour, as Graham was constrained to return on board his ship ; such is the rigour of discipline !

General Lake had now to perform the dis- tressful duty of making examples of some of . the most iniquitous conspirators ; and courts- martial were summoned to try them. Roche, a catholic priest, was among the most ardent of those rebel chiefs, and was found guilty. He had impiously abandoned his holy office to carry a pike ; and commanded the bands of insurgents who fought at Fook's Mill. Keough, the counterfeit Governor of Wex-

ford at the time the murders were perpetrated, was the next in conspicuous infamy.
When led to execution, he requested permission from Brigadier Moore to address the
people.

This being granted, he declared aloud *,
' that he had never been an United Irishman.
' In the early part of his life (he said) he had
' served in the army, and had never then, nor
' since, deviated from the path of honour.
' Now as he was about to appear before his
' Redeemer, it was not likely that he should
' assert what was false; and he positively
' declared that he never was concerned in
' any plot or conspiracy against the King
' or the Constitution of his country; but,
' on the contrary, that previous to the rebels
' taking Wexford, he had exerted himself
' against them in its defence. After the
' King's forces retreated, and the rebels, to
' the amount of twenty thousand, entered,
' they compelled him, at the point of their
' pikes, to be their commander; and in that

* Journal, MS.

' compulsory office he had acted with hu-
' manity.'

He spoke with so much firmness and apparent truth, that Moore was greatly moved.
He whispered to the officer who was charged
with the executions, to delay; and to take
care that this should be the last. He then
ran to General Lake, and told him what had
passed. The General thanked him, and replied, that it was natural he should be affected by so solemn a denial. But he assured Moore, that he had seen a number of
Keough's intercepted letters to the other
chiefs, which were of the most horrible description; and it was completely ascertained
that he had been a principal leader in the
rebellion. Notwithstanding this, the clergyman who attended the impenitent criminal to
the gallows, told Moore, that he had persevered until death in denying his guilt; and
his conduct was such, that he had not offered
him the last sacrament. It may appear
strange, that he did not ultimately seek for
consolation in confession and repentance;

but falsehood is the cloak usually put on to hide wickedness, and the most obdurate never cast it off, from the fear of shame.

The British Minister, anxious to put a termination to these miserable scenes in Ireland, sent thither Earl Cornwallis, a humane nobleman, skilled in civil and military affairs. On his arrival at Dublin, the rebellion being suppressed, he issued a proclamation of the most conciliatory nature. The people were exhorted to lay down their arms and return to their homes, and their work; and assurances given, that if they remained tranquil, they would be protected. The orders issued to the army were in accordance with this pacific design, in the hope of composing the frenzy of the people.

Brigadier Moore was at this period promoted to the rank of Major-General, and the number of troops placed under his command were augmented. It became his duty to wait upon Lord Cornwallis, and he went to Dublin for that purpose. This much-experienced general and statesman behaved to him with singular regard, and conversed familiarly, as if of long acquaintance. He inquired particularly of the conduct of the Irish militia and yeomanry, both in the field and in quarters ; and of Irish affairs in general. To the information solicited, he gave an attentive ear; and at the conclusion of the conference informed Moore, that he meant his corps to be a moving body, and always ready to be sent to whatever point danger or commotion was threatened.

Moore had several other interviews with the Lord Lieutenant, who had greatly retrenched the usual pomp and ceremony of the court. Moore remarked his plain demeanour, the solid sense of his conversation, and his judicious method of transacting business. As soon as his affairs were arranged, he took his leave and returned to Blessington, where his corps was assembled. The armies of the rebels had all been defeated, but considerable numbers of refractory men, entertaining hopes of aid from France, still persevered in hostilities. Large bodies of them lurked in the mountains and glens of Wicklow; from which they frequently issued, and spread devastation around. Moore was employed against them, and first tried by mild means to restore peace; but some of the gentry and yeomanry were so highly ex- asperated by the murder of their relatives, and the injuries they had suffered, that they were too much disposed to retaliation. This he restrained by his counsel and authority; and spread widely the Lord Lieutenant's hu- mane proclamation. He himself spoke to the country people, always with kindness, recommended them to give up their arms, and assured them of good treatment, if they would return to their occupations, and reside at home. By these means, in a very short time, upwards of twelve hundred men sur- rendered their arms, and sought for protec- tions; which being granted, others crowded in daily for the same purpose. But as, in the hot-bed of civil war, vices multiply and attain maturity, there still remained hordes of irreclaimable rebels, meditating vengeance,

Many of these lay in wait in the mountains of Wicklow, and in boggy places, from whence they issued to plunder and burn property, murder the farmers and proprietors, and wage a cruel desultory war. Moore drew up a plan to put an end to these heinous deeds, which he carried to Dublin, and laid before the Lord Lieutenant. This being approved of, he proceeded to put it in execution.

In order to occupy a wider range of country, he divided his troops into four parties. The commandants of each received orders to keep up, as they advanced, a regular communication with each other,—to preserve strict discipline,—and to prevent the soldiers from injuring the unarmed inhabitants, who were to be treated amicably.

He then moved forward against the rebels, who were active and vigilant. They rarely attempted open resistance, cunningly evading all attacks; but fired from covers, flew from hill to hill, from fastness to fastness, and escaped across the bogs by narrow paths,

known only to themselves. The pursuit was
rendered very harassing by continued rains;
and Moore, as well as the soldiers, slept on
the ground without even a tent. He gave
his enemies no respite; he occupied the villages and glens where they might procure
·food; pushed on wherever they assembled,
chased them from their hidden holds, and
kept them continually on foot. This cease-
less flight becoming insupportable, some
threw away their arms and dispersed; but
the greater number submitted, and solicited
protections, which were still held out to them.
In three weeks the country was quieted, and
the inhabitants at their work; but the fatigue
endured threw General Moore into a fever,
which confined him seven days in his tent.
Lord Cornwallis, hearing of his illness, despatched instantly his own physician to
attend him; and Moore, when enabled to
travel, went to Dublin, to obtain some respite
from affairs. Yet, before his health was fully
re-established, he was summoned to the
Castle, and found Lord Cornwallis examining

busily a large map of Ireland. He told Moore he had just received intelligence that the French had landed, and showed him the letters. The numbers of the French did not appear to be great, yet this was indistinctly stated; while it was clearly announced that their reception by the Irish was most cordial.

Lord Cornwallis was well aware of the evil disposition and thirst for revenge, which prevailed through the country so recently subjected; and that multitudes were eager to rise in insurrection again, should the slightest hopes of success appear, or more disembarkations from France take place. He discussed the subject with Moore; and as he possessed both prudence and fortitude, and was also habituated to business, he formed his arrangements with promptitude. General Lake was despatched to Galway, to assemble the troops in that vicinity, but was . positively ordered not to engage the enemy until he had collected a force large enough to ensure success. Similar instructions were despatched elsewhere;

and Moore was directed to march with his division to Salins, to embark it in boats, and sail along the canal to Tullamore, and from thence proceed to Athlone.

This town was the central place of rendezvous for the principal army, which Lord Cornwallis resolved to command in person. Orders were also transmitted to the commandants of corps throughout Ireland, to be on their guard, and by vigilance to overawe the disaffected. At four o'clock in the morning, Moore moved off from Blessington at the head of his troops, and reached Salins before boats on the canal were procured. Lord Cornwallis arrived there at noon; when all embarked, sailed to Tullamore, and then marched rapidly to Kilbiggen.

Advice was there received of the advance of other corps towards Athlone; but his Lordship expressed to Moore great uneasiness at General Hutchinson having proceeded with a small force to Castlebar, much too near the enemy, as it would be highly imprudent to risk an action when reinforcements were so near. This apprehension was soon verified; for next day, on reaching Athlone, advice was brought that the French and rebels had traversed the mountains which were unguarded, and had suddenly attacked the corps near Castlebar. General Lake had arrived the night before, and assumed the command. His troops were almost all Irish militia, who after a slight resistance, to his astonishment, took to flight, and no efforts of his could stop them. Cannon, ammunition, and baggage, were all abandoned; and many of the prisoners who were taken, enlisted with the enemy.

This defeat, which manifested disaffection among the Irish militia, and the multitudes of malecontents that flocked to join the French, rendered the state of affairs very serious. Lake collected the fugitives at Tuam, above sixty miles from the field of battle, and Colonel Crawford was detached with a corps of cavalry to patrole near Castlebar, and procure good intelligence; for the reports of the country people were uniformly false. The army then moved forward to Ballinamore, where they halted one day for the arrival of more troops of a species that might be relied on. Several British regiments of the line, together with some good regiments of English and Scottish militia, then came up: the whole were formed into three brigades, and the command of the reserve, three thousand strong, was assigned to Moore.

I shall now digress from public affairs to notice, that an exaggerated report of General Moore's illness at Wexford had reached London, and thrown his family into consternation. I asked, and obtained my father's consent to pass over into Ireland to take charge of my brother's health. I then set off for Dublin, and found there a messenger going with despatches to the Lord-Lieutenant; I got admittance into his chaise, and by travelling night and day, overtook the army at Newton-Mount-Bellew. It was in the middle of a fine star-light night, when we approached the camp; a sentinel challenged us; the messenger gave the pass-word, and

we were permitted to enter. The army, with
the exception of the guards and pickets, was
reposing in tents. We were conducted to
a house in which Lord Cornwallis slept : a
surrounding guard was on the alert, but
encumbered the passages and staircases.
Through these soldiers fast asleep, the
messenger with his despatches, was conducted to the Earl's bed-chamber. A staff-
officer inquired who I was; and on communicating my name and business, he
directed a dragoon to take up my portman-
teau on his horse, and conduct me to the
reserve, which was encamped upwards of a
mile in front. I was led over a wild heath,
and by the rising dawn, saw the summit of a
ridge of hills at no great distance.

The dragoon told me that the reserve was
posted there. As we ascended, the light increased, and the morning gun was fired, followed by the sound of trumpets, bugle-horns,
pipes, drums, and fifes, playing the *reveille.*
Tents instantly were struck, and a line of infantry and cavalry appeared, drawn out in

battalia. The dragoon inquired for General
Moore; he was directed to the left of the line,
to which we proceeded, and saw a table-cloth,
with a breakfast apparatus, spread on the
grass. Seven or eight officers sat around,
among whom was my brother. Seeing me,
he sprang up with glad surprise, and clasped
my hand. ' Well, James! have you come
' to see a battle? " I came to bring you
' health to fight one; but your looks show
' that you've got it already. Yet, when
' blows are near at hand, a surgeon dropping
' in may not be superfluous."'

He then introduced me to Lord Huntley
and his aides-de-camp, who were enjoying
a substantial meal with soldiers' appetites.

When breakfast was despatched, a horse
was procured for me, and the march began.
The day was fine, and this advanced corps
was composed of light and heavy dragoons,
of German hussars whose horses were gaily
caparisoned, of English and Irish infantry,
artillery, and Scottish Highlanders, in all
their variegated uniforms.

The view of the column was very striking, now ascending the heathy hills, then descending the valleys in long array, with glittering arms, and with all that martial pomp and ceremony, which is so captivating to the ambitious. Before the army halted, I was exceedingly tired, and rested in a tent. Not so my brother, whose labours seemed then only to commence. He galloped all round the country, examined every wood, and eminence, questioned the country people respecting every road and path, and compared their different accounts with a good map. He then posted pickets and patroles to guard each avenue to the camp, and appointed the ground where every corps should form, in case of an alarm by night or by day. Until these arrangements were completed, he neither rested nor dined. After a brief meal, he rode out again, to see that all his orders had been punctually obeyed, and the camp in order; he then waited upon Lord Cornwallis, whose confidence he enjoyed, and who communicated to him all the intelligence he had received. It was ascertained that the French were still lying at Castlebar, arming and training the Irish. The reports of the numbers of the enemy were strangely contradictory; some of the country people gave assurances that they were few in number, others swore positively to their exceeding twenty thousand men. To ascertain the truth was impossible; but it afterwards appeared, that only eleven hundred French soldiers had landed; that the Irish, who joined them in succession, were very numerous; but many, disheartened by seeing the small number of the French, quitted them, and that not above five thousand actually remained.

The conference at head-quarters continued late, and I growing sleepy, wrapped myself up in my great coat, and lay down on a blanket spread on a truss of straw. Before dropping asleep, my brother arrived, wished me good night; then pulling off his boots only, he stretched himself on another truss of straw, and slept soundly. At break of day, a sentinel, and the *reveille*, broke our slumbers; when my brother started up, and mounted his charger. I was warned that the tent must be struck, and was forced to creep from under my blanket, and to get on horseback also. The morning proved raw; rain poured the whole day, and the army, after a march of six hours, halted on a bleak marshy moor. Being thoroughly wet, and shivering with cold, I found a canvas tent, without a fire, a comfortless resting-place; yet my brother did not allow himself that shelter, repose, or food, until the soldiers were provided for, the guards planted, and all the precautions requisite for the security of the camp settled. The delusions which I had previously formed, of the delights of glorious war, were now somewhat damped: for I perceived that a general who exerts himself to the utmost, independent of incessant mental occupation, must frequently endure more bodily labour than a private soldier.

While the French and rebels remained at Castlebar there was no need of precipitation, therefore Lord Cornwallis advanced slowly, giving time for the junction of several regiments, who were on their march : and he detached General Lake to the little town of Boyle, to keep watch on that quarter; while the principal army, exceeding ten thousand men, arrived at Holy Mount. It was then resolved to march, on the following morning, to Castlebar, ten miles distant, and Moore was commanded to storm the town with the reserve, which would be supported by the rest of the army.

I had now the conviction that I should be present at a battle, the brunt of which would be sustained by my brother. The disposition was fixed; when in the evening Lord Cornwallis sent for Moore, and informed him that the French and rebels had evacuated Castlebar; but no one could give any account of their route. He was much disconcerted with this vague intelligence; and he had also learned that risings had begun in the counties of Longford and Westmeath. Colonel Crawford was immediately ordered to pro-

ceed to Castlebar, and to follow the enemy
with a detachment of dragoons; and General
Lake to pursue the same track, to harass
and detain them, but not to risk an action.
He determined himself to march eastward, to
Ballyhannis, lest the French should cross the
Shannon, and endeavour to throw themselves
into the above disaffected counties; or by a
rapid movement, gain the advance, and reach
Dublin before him. But on arriving at Ballyhannis, information was received that the
enemy had taken a northerly course, towards
Sligo; probably, because they expected on
that coast a fresh disembarkation from
France: Crawford and Lake were in rapid
pursuit. Moore was then detached in aid of
Lake, whose force was believed to be much
less numerous than that of the enemy; and
Lord Cornwallis proceeded in haste towards
the Shannon, always to interpose his army
between the French and the capital. As
the enemy had no baggage, and were excellent marchers, it was difficult to keep pace

with them. Although on horseback I was
sadly fatigued, and pitied the soldiers, loaded
with their heavy knapsacks and arms, climb-
ing up the hills, and completing twenty-five
miles, or more, daily.

The French reached Coloony without being
overtaken; but they were there met by three ·
hundred of the Limerick militia, commanded
by Colonel Vereker. This officer had advanced from Sligo, with this insufficient corps,
without orders. He was repulsed, lost two
pieces of cannon, and a number of prisoners.

This was a second triumph for the French,
which was resounded through the country in
order to encourage insurrection. The action,
however, delayed the enemy half a day.
Moore reached Coloony next morning, closely
following Lake; and while we were pushing
forward with tired troops, an express came
from Lord Cornwallis to alter our course,
because the French had altered their's, and
were directing their march towards him.
Moore was, therefore, ordered to turn towards

Boyle and Carrick, to support Lord Cornwallis, who had crossed the Shannon at Carrick.

The French and rebels passed that river
higher to the north, at Ballintra; and a party
of Irish were left to destroy the bridge. But
this work was interrupted by Colonel Crawford's dragoons, who dashed over, and sabred
many. The dragoons continued to hang on
the enemy's rear, harassing and delaying
them, until Lake came up, and stopped their
further flight. The French being overtaken,
drew up, and, after one discharge, grounded
their arms. Quarter was given them, but
great numbers of the rebels were shot on the
field.

General Humbert, the French commander,
was so beset that he could not escape; for
Lord Cornwallis had reached St. Johnstone
on his right flank, and Moore's corps was
hastening to Carrick. When the news of the
successful issue came to us, a grievous lamen-
tation was made by the officers and soldiers,

who had toiled after the French in vain ; but
Moore said, ' 'Tis better that it should have
' fallen to the lot of General Lake to capture
' Humbert, who had triumphed over him at
' Castlebar.'   As, however, I was not present
at the catastrophe of the rebellion, I returned
to London disappointed.

The measures adopted by the Lord Lieutenant were criticised as usual by many ca-
villers, who asserted that against so small a
French force they were cautious to excess.
But General Moore, knowing the hostile disposition of the Irish Catholics, approved entirely of Lord Cornwallis's conduct, which he
considered judiciously circumspect, and calculated to prevent an imminent calamity.

The Earl intended to send Moore to
retake Kilala ; but despatches arrived from
London, intimating that a French armament,
at Brest, was preparing to sail for Ireland.
Moore was in consequence detained, an augmented force was put under his command,
with which he encamped in a central position

near Athlone; with orders to hold himself in readiness to march against the enemy wherever they landed.

The rebel garrison in Kilala, having time given them, might easily have saved themselves; but with absurd pertinacity they remained in the place until a detachment arrived, under General Trench, which completely routed them. They had been in expectation of aid from France, and there was perhaps no negligence in the French ministry, who were sufficiently desirous of keeping alive the flame of rebellion in Ireland; but the sea, and the British cruisers, hindered their measures from being well combined. Yet before the assault of Kilala, a French brig, with arms and a few soldiers, did arrive at Donegal. A noted Irish agitator, named Napper Tandy, was on board; who having learnt that Humbert's corps was captured, he published a pompous proclamation, and sailed back to France.

This essay was, however, followed quickly by another alarm. A French fleet con-

sisting of an eighty-four-gun ship and eight
large frigates, appeared in the beginning of
October, off the North coast of Ireland.
Four thousand troops were embarked in this
fleet, whose landing was prevented by the
sudden approach of a British squadron, commanded by Sir John Borlase Warren. A
fierce conflict ensued: in which the line-of-
battle-ship, and three of the frigates, struck
their colours ; the remaining frigates separated
and took to flight.   My brother Graham,
commanding the Melampus frigate, was hotly
engaged in this action.   The chase continued
all night, and next morning only two of the
frigates were in sight, these the Admiral continued in pursuit of; but directed Captain
Moore to examine the bay of Killibeg, where
it was suspected one of the enemy might
have taken shelter.   At midnight, he descried close within shore two large vessels
of the enemy.   He bore up to them, engaged
a ship carrying forty guns and four hundred
men, which struck to him; and the other
sheered off in the dark.   After taking pos-

prize, as he foresaw an approaching storm, he steered for the Clyde, where he rode in safety: by which nautical prescience, he shunned a hurricane which shattered and had nearly foundered the rest of the squadron. Among the prisoners who were taken was Wolfe Tone, the prime fomenter of the Irish rebellion. This man had once before been arrested for treason; but by dissembled repentance his forfeited life had been spared by government. On this occasion he tried to escape by legal chicanery; which failing, with his own hand he finished his pernicious life.

Chapter IX.

DEPARTURE FROM IRELAND—CAMPAIGN IN HOLLAND.

The defeat of the French invaders, and the punishment of the rebels, pacified Ireland. But this temporary benefit was procured by a British army, which put an end to a calamitous insurrection raised on the fallacious plea of liberty.

Were all mankind disinclined to injure or do injustice to each other, they certainly ought to be left to the enjoyment of perfect liberty, and every man should have the power of acting as he pleased. But the dispositions and habits of human beings to do unto others, what they would not that others do unto them, render the establishment of laws and government essential for their welfare.

As the prevalence of vice is the only good cause for imposing any restraints on freedom, these never should be greater than is requisite for the happiness of the people; and always proportioned to their disposition to do evil. The degrees of virtue, and the tendency to various vices, are different in different countries; consequently one code of laws, and one constitution of government, are unsuitable to all. Projects of one universal legislative system would neither be agreeable to the tempers, nor adapted to the correction of the various corruptions, of the human race. Experience proves this.

The English laws and constitution have been found admirably suited to the character of Englishmen: which imposed upon them no greater prohibitions than were requisite for establishing good order; and which granted a greater degree of freedom than was possessed by any other nation.

In the year 1706, this constitution was extended to Scotland, and suddenly the Scots were transformed from an ill-governed, turbulent, and impoverished people, into an orderly, composed, and improving nation: which concordant effects proved that there was an agreement in character, and an equality in morals with the English.

But when the same constitution was transferred to Ireland, no such beneficial consequences ensued; for lawless riots, wanton pillagings, and atrocious murders have continued to prevail in that hapless country. And it is found absolutely necessary to maintain there a numerous standing army, to restrain carnage and the destruction of property from increasing throughout the island.

The continuance of these flagrant acts is a decisive proof that the restrictions of the laws and constitution are not proportioned to the propensity to do wrong. If the freedom of the Irish laws and government were wisely graduated by the scale of virtue and morals which have been attained by the natives, it is reasonable to believe that they would soon become peaceful, prosperous, and happy.

Under the just administration of Earl Corn-wallis, whose authority was maintained by a considerable military force, the turmoils of Ireland were respited. He sent for General Moore to come to Dublin on public affairs ; apartments were assigned to him ; and he was treated by his Lordship as a friend. In the course of Moore's diversified life he could not avoid contracting the enmity of a few persons of dubious and vicious characters ; but he was esteemed and beloved by all those with whom he had intercourse, who were themselves eminent for virtue and pa-triotism.

Towards the close of the year 1798, an expedition to the Mediterranean was pro-jected, the command of which was given to Sir Charles Stuart. A correspondent at Head-quarters wrote to Moore, that it was under consideration to employ him, if he chose it, on this enterprise. But an objec-tion occurred to Moore to the acceptance of this proposal, from a delicacy he felt towards the Lord-Lieutenant.

Earl Cornwallis was a downright, sensible man, and a contemner of ceremony. He distinguished Moore by his friendship; who felt so much gratitude for the treatment he had received, that he would not express to his correspondent at the Horse-Guards a wish to leave Ireland, even for a foreign service which he coveted.

A second confidential, letter soon after, signified, 'That the subject had been dis-
' cussed by the Duke of York and Mr. Dun-
' das, the Secretary of War; when the latter
' said, " That Lord Cornwallis in his private
' " correspondence, laid so much stress upon
' " the esteem he had for General Moore,
' " that he did not think he could be removed
' " without giving Lord Cornwallis umbrage."
' The intention is, therefore, for the present
' at least, given up.'

The next year, 1799, the war took a favourable turn. Buonaparte was repulsed at St. Jean D'Acre, and had retreated into Egypt; and Suwarrow, with a Russian army, was victorious in Italy. The British War-

Minister conceived that this was a propitious opportunity for rescuing Holland from the thraldom of France. And if the Dutch at that time had retained the same love of liberty and independence, which they had displayed in the sixteenth century, against Spain, or in the seventeenth against France, the plan would undoubtedly have succeeded. It was formed on an extensive scale: near seventeen thousand Russians were subsidised, who, together with a considerable British army, were to be embarked on this expedition.

The delay which must have occurred by attempting to transport so large a force at once, induced the minister to embark ten thousand British troops, led by Sir Ralph Abercombie, to be landed in Holland in the first place; and the remaining forces were to be transported afterwards, as quickly as the means of conveyance could be procured.

No sooner was this enterprise concerted, than Moore received a summons from Lord Cornwallis, who informed him that his

presence was required in England by the
·ministers ; and his Lordship gave him a
letter to Mr. Dundas, in which he thus expressed himself:

‘ June 21, 1799.

‘ I am sure you know me too well to sus-
‘ pect that any selfish consideration can
‘ weigh a moment with me against the general
‘ interests of the country.

‘ You shall have all the troops you ask,
‘ and General Moore ; who is a greater loss
‘ to me than the troops. But he will be of
‘ infinite service to Abercrombie : and I
‘ likewise think it an object to the state, that
‘ an officer of his talents and character should
‘ have every opportunity of acquiring know-
‘ ledge and experience in his profession*.’

Moore crossed the channel, and his family
were gratified by his presence only for a few
days. For he was immediately appointed to
the command of a brigade of troops encamped
on the coast of Hampshire. To this camp

* This extract was sent to Dr. Moore by the Secretary of State.

he repaired, and the various regiments intended for embarkation assembled in succession. As the greater part of the troops were raw soldiers, and little acquainted with many essential parts of their business, he seized the opportunity of exercising and instructing them in this encampment. And to render them expert in pitching and striking their tents, and in manœuvring, he marched them along the coast from Barham Downs, encamping them every night, instead of quartering them in the towns and villages.

This was the commencement of the formation of that army, which was afterwards so distinguished in various campaigns.

It was in the beginning of August, that a fleet of transports was collected at Ramsgate, in which the troops were speedily embarked, and sailed forthwith. The landing was intended to be made in the island of Goree, at the mouth of the Meuse; whence the troops might cross over to the Isle of Overflakkee, and proceed forward, if practicable, into the heart of the United Provinces.

But storms arose, which rendered it dangerous to approach the coast.   On the 21st of
August, the weather becoming fine, the
general officers were assembled in Admiral
Mitchell's ship.   They were informed that,
in consequence of the difficulties of landing
at Goree, the Admiral and Sir Ralph had
abandoned that design, and had resolved to
attack the Texel, opposite to which the fleet
was then lying.   In the mean time, a flag of
truce was sent in to summon the Dutch fleet
to surrender.   But that evening it blew so
hard, that Admiral Mitchell was obliged to
sail off, and could not return for a week,
which gave the enemy time for preparation.

On the morning of the 27th, the landing
was effected with a great deal of confusion.
General Moore got first on shore with only
about three hundred men of different regiments.   He was opposed by the enemy's
pickets, whom he repulsed.   In about half
an hour, the whole of his brigade got on shore,
with which he advanced, drove back the
enemy, and drew up his troops in front of the

entrenchments-of the Helder. Sir James
Pulteney landed with two brigades on his
right to the south, and advancing over the
sand-hills, fell in with a large body of the
enemy. The contest became brisk, when
Sir Ralph, with the grenadiers of the
Guards, moved to his assistance; and the
enemy were repelled.

When the action was over, Sir Ralph visited Moore's position, and gave orders that
he should storm the Helder that very night.
By deserters, who came in, it was ascertained
that there were actually in the Helder two
thousand soldiers. Towards the evening,
Moore observed some movement among the
enemy's troops, and before it was quite dark
he saw them marching off on the road to Alkmaar. He advanced to the works, when a
flag of truce appeared, bringing proposals to
surrender the Helder. Immediately he moved
forward, and took possession of the town.

In the morning, when the British troops
were seen occupying the batteries which
commanded the harbour, the Dutch fleet

slipped their cables to escape. They were chased by the British fleet, and, being over-taken, surrendered. Whoever reflects on the use which might have been made of this fleet so near to the English coast, by an en-terprising enemy, must consider this capture as a most important advantage.

While the cannon and stores were disem-barking, Sir Ralph obtained certain intelli-gence, that the forces of the enemy, collected at Alkmaar, amounted to five thousand French and eight thousand Dutch, which were augmenting daily. It, therefore, be-came necessary to take up a defensive posi-tion, and wait for the reinforcements which were coming.

In the meantime, proclamations were is-sued, to assure the Dutch nation that this invasion was undertaken, not for conquest, but with the friendly design of delivering Holland from the servile yoke of France; and all patriotic Dutchmen were exhorted to rise up in arms to emancipate their country. But the spirit of the people, depressed by their conquerors, could not be roused. The Dutch troops, which formed the most numerous part of the enemy's army, served slavishly under the orders of the French General, and fought against those who came to emancipate them. The character of these Dutchmen was very different from that of their ancestors, who had resisted pertinaciously the sanguinary Duke of Alva, the heroic Condé and Turenne, and had inundated their country, rather than submit to foreign subjection.

As the forces of the French General were constantly accumulating, he only engaged in slight skirmishes, until a fleet appeared off the coast, bringing reinforcements to the British. He then determined to attack the lines, in expectation of driving the invaders into the sea, before these reinforcements should land. During the night of the 9th September unusual noises were heard by the outlying pickets. At day-break, Moore with his usual vigilance, sent out a patrole of dragoons, and rode himself to the advanced posts to reconnoitre.

There was scarcely light, yet he saw through
the haze great masses of soldiers approaching.   Instantly his aide-de-camp, Anderson,
was despatched to the pickets, and all the
regiments of his division were ordered to
their alarm posts.   A smart firing soon began,
and the pickets fell back behind a canal;
when Anderson, with the presence of mind of
an experienced officer, got the bridges taken
up, as soon as the soldiers had passed over.

The enemy's light troops and riflemen,
covering themselves by the inequalities of
the ground, pushed forward; some pieces of
artillery were also advanced, and a brisk fire
kept up.   This was answered only by scattered
shots from a few light infantry, as Moore's
brigade lay concealed behind a dyke.   At
length a large solid column of the enemy,
raising a loud shout, while drums and bugle
horns sounded the charge, rushed on with
impetuosity,   The British sprang up by command, and threw in a well-directed volley,
which, together with grape-shot from the field
artillery, mounted on the dyke, astounded

the enemy, who drew back in confusion.
The attacks on other parts of the line were
also unsuccessful; yet one column carried a
village and a redoubt, but could penetrate no
farther; for the stout resistance which the
enemy met with, compelled them to retreat
on all points, and they were pursued for some
distance by the reserve.

At the commencement of this action, a
shot grazed General Moore's hand, and struck
his spy-glass; the brass-mounting turned
the ball, which otherwise must have passed
through his body.   On that evening the
Duke of York landed at the Helder to as-
sume the command; and in the two following days, the Russian and British reinforcements disembarked, augmenting the army to
thirty-four thousand men.

It was an unfortunate measure to send
a young prince, though endowed with a
warm and beneficent heart together with
a good understanding, to take the chief
command from Sir Ralph Abercrombie,
who had been trained to arms from early

life. The position of the army, on a
hostile shore, opposed to a skilful French
General, required a leader of consummate
experience to foresee and overcome all the
obstacles and stratagems which were to be
expected. The King's partiality to his gallant son was natural; but the cabinet council being unprepossessed, instead of appointing this ambitious youth to the superintend-
ance, ought assuredly to have placed him
under the guidance of the veteran general.

The disembarkation of the newly arrived
force took place at the Helder; and Sir
Ralph Abercrombie, now commanding only
the left wing of the army, moved forward.
Moore's brigade was flanked by the Zuyder
Zee, and his advanced pickets were close to
those of the enemy. Every preparation
having been completed, it was resolved by
the Duke of York to make a general assault
on the enemy's lines. The Russians were
drawn up on the right wing and entrusted
with the principal attack; as his Royal
Highness entertained high confidence in

their valour ; and this was augmented by the boastful pretensions of their commander General D'Herman, who declined all sup- port, asserting positively that nothing could withstand his Russians. The central columns were led by General Dundas, and the left wing by Sir James Pulteney.

As the Duke of York had no doubt of the success of the attack, he detached on the evening before the battle Sir Ralph Aber- crombie with ten thousand men, to march by the shore of the Zuyder Zee, to the town of Hoorn, to turn the enemy's right flank, get into their rear, and intercept them when de- feated.

Conformably to his orders, Sir Ralph moved off in the evening with Moore's brigade, and two others, together with a con- siderable train of artillery. He reached Hoorn at one in the morning, and took the garrison, amounting to two hundred men, pri- soners. The night was rainy and boisterous, and by the long march over rough roads, and broken bridges, the soldiers were exceedingly harassed. They were directed to lie down on their arms upon the road, as Sir Ralph waited, before he advanced farther, until he should have tidings of the other columns. He remained long without any certain intelligence; though, from hearing the report of cannon, he knew that the battle raged. The Russians had advanced early in the morning with ardour and irregularity. They bravely broke the enemy's first line, and carried the village of Berghen, but preserved no order. When dispersed, and in confusion, they were attacked by a fresh corps of the enemy, and absolutely routed. D'Herman and another General were captured. Great numbers of the Russians were killed collectedly, or dispersedly, as they resisted or fled. But to check the pursuit, the British Guards and other troops from the nearest column were ordered to their aid. On the left Sir James Pulteney's column carried the enemy's lines and batteries, against which he had been directed, with judgment and success; yet in consequence of the defeat of the Russians he was recalled, and in such haste, as to be obliged to abandon all the cannon he had taken. At length an aide-de-camp on a reeking horse, brought the bad news to Sir Ralph Abercrombie, with an order to return immediately to rejoin the Duke of York. Sir Ralph rode off, leaving Moore to lead back the column; which, after a long and wearisome march, took up their former ground.

This retreat of the army was directed in consequence of the alarm caused by the flight of the Russians; but was perhaps unnecessary. For, as Sir James Pulteney had defeated the enemy's right wing, and was master of their cannon, he could easily have maintained that advanced position: and if he had been reinforced with Sir Ralph Abercrombie's troops, the conjoined force could have fallen upon the enemy's flank, and might have entirely changed the fortune of the day.

The loss of the Russians in killed, wounded, and captured amounted to near three thousand men; and that of the British to about fifteen hundred. Yet the loss of the enemy was greater ; of whom three thousand were made prisoners, chiefly Dutchmen. The Russians were much disheartened by this disaster ; yet the Duke of York resolved to make another effort to penetrate into the country. With this design, he nearly reversed his former order of battle ; assigning to Sir Ralph Abercrombie's column the hardest task, that of forcing those posts from which the Russians had been beaten in the former action.

Some days were spent in making preparations for the second engagement; and tempestuous weather increased the delay, until September 29th: when General Moore's brigade, at three o'clock in the morning, was moved forward to begin the attack. But after marching a short distance, he was recalled, much to the discontent of the soldiers; it having been discovered that owing to high winds, the strand over which he was to pass was flooded by the sea. Moore was glad of this counter order, as he had been affected for two days with an attack of fever, which he concealed. On returning to his tent, powerful febrifuge medicines were administered, which cured him.

October 2nd was finally fixed upon for the onset. The British were drawn up on the right and left wings, and the Russians in the centre. Two British corps were also formed in the rear of the Russians, and of the left wing, to support them. The plan of the battle was, that Sir Ralph Abercrombie's column, which formed the right wing, should commence by advancing upon the enemy's left wing, to repel and turn it: so the success of the day entirely depended upon this attack. At six o'clock in the morning, Moore, to whom Sir Ralph gave the command of his advanced guard, marched forward on the beach; and the Duke of York saw him pass. He first fell in with some pickets whom he chased away. On approaching the enemy's line, he observed that the corps termed the reserve, which had been directed to proceed on his right flank, had wandered away to the left. This was a serious mistake, as his right was

thereby exposed. The enemy seized the advantage, pushed on a body of troops in that
direction, who kept up a galling fire both on
his front and flank; but his soldiers, inspired with animation, charged boldly and
repulsed the enemy. In this assault Moore
was shot through the thigh, but not dis-
abled. Fresh troops of the enemy were
quickly brought up, who pressed on his
front, and lurked on his flank, taking post
on the sand-hills, and wherever the ground
favoured them. Moore, relying on himself,
sometimes detached parties to clear his
flanks, sometimes stood firm pouring volleys
of shot on his foes; and charged them with
bayonets, whenever the opportunity offered.

For five hours he continued advancing and
repelling successive corps of the enemy, who
defended fiercely every inch of ground. Towards the evening after having his horse killed
under him, and being lame from his wound,
he approached the village of Egmont op Zee,
still driving the enemy before him. By this
time, his troops, greatly reduced in number,

were exhausted with the fatigue of fighting
and marching over rugged ground and sinking sand.   Many overcome with lassitude
had fallen behind, and the rest were scattered
and out of order.   In this emergency the
French reserve, in a long compact line,
moved up against him.   Moore tried in vain
to make his men charge them; when, seeing they were too few to resist this numerous fresh corps, he despatched his aide-de-
camp, Anderson, to bring up the Gordon
Highlanders, the regiment nearest at hand.
But before their arrival, the enemy came on
boldly; they nearly surrounded his thinned
ranks and discharged upon them a destructive fire, which was faintly returned.   He
saw his men falling fast around him, and on
the point of giving way, when he was struck
by a ball, which entered the cheek, and came
out behind the ear.   He fell to the ground
stunned, and felt as if the side of his head
had been carried off.   He concluded that he
was mortally wounded, and lay without either
the power or inclination to stir, glad to find

it was so easy to die. He soon heard a soldier say, ' There is our General, let us carry ' him with us ;' and he was raised from the ground. He then opened his eyes, and saw that the enemy were close upon him ; on which he made a strong effort, and by the help of a soldier was hurried to the rear, passing through the advancing line of Highlanders. His retiring troops rallied around this reinforcement, and returned to the charge with renewed spirit. They attacked and drove back the French reserve with considerable slaughter. The battle was then won, though some skirmishing occurred in the evening, and an attempt was made by the enemy's cavalry to regain two pieces of cannon : but this was frustrated by a gallant charge made by Lord Paget, with a few light dragoons and a number of officers who accompanied him. In the whole of this hard-fought action, Sir Ralph Abercrombie exposed himself much : he had two horses shot under him, and his column discomfited all the troops which fronted them. But the reports he received from the other columns were dubious; he could not learn whether the Russians had penetrated to Berghen, or where they were. So the aged, wearied-out General, after posting his troops on the best station he could find, instead of sleeping on a good bed, laid himself down on a wet sand-hill without a tent; and passed a miserable night from cold and anxiety.

But next morning the good news was brought him, that the centre and left wing, which had encountered less resistance, had also repelled their adversaries. For when the French General found that his left was completely turned, he drew back all his forces, and the Duke of York entered and took possession of Berghen and Alkmaer, which towns were the fruits of the victory.

An act of kindness of Sir Ralph Abercrombie on this occasion shall be noticed. Foreseeing the alarm and distress which the accounts of the action would raise in General Moore's family, he wrote the following letter from the field of battle to Dr. Moore :—

' Egmond-on-the-Sea, Oct. 4th.

' My dear Sir,

' Although your son is wounded in the
' thigh, and in the cheek, I can assure you
' he is in no sort of danger ; both wounds
' are slight.   The public and myself are the
' greatest sufferers by these accidents.

' The General is a hero, with more sense
' than many others of that description.   In
' that he is an ornament to his family, and
' to his profession.   I hope Mrs. Moore and
' his sister will be easy on his account, and
' that you are proud of such a son.

' Your's,

' RALPH ABERCROMBIE.'

Moore was helped from the field to the
rear, where his wounds were drest ; he was
then lifted on a horse, led by his groom, and
conveyed back to his quarters, near ten miles
distant.   This journey he sustained with
great difficulty, being exhausted with his
exertions through the day, and faint from
great loss of blood.

While he was confined to his bed, on account of his wounds, an incident occurred which might have proved fatal. Inflammation having spread around the wound through the cheek, the surgeons bathed the part with a strong solution of sugar-of-lead, and whey was recommended to him as a refreshing beverage. These two liquids were of a similar colour, and his servant one day, instead of the whey, placed the lotion near his bedside : and when the General awoke from sleep, being thirsty, he took the bason which contained the poisonous solution, and swallowed it. He instantly discovered the mistake he had committed, called for his friend Anderson, who was in an adjoining room, and calmly told him what he had done ; then, with that presence of mind which never forsook him, asked for a feathered pen he saw on the writing-stand. Anderson gave it him, and ran off for an oil cruet and water ; by means of these he quickly threw the poison out of his stomach.

When sufficiently recovered to be removed

he was carried to the Helder, embarked in a frigate for England, and returned to the bosom of his family. His mother, transported to see him once more brought home alive, nursed him with the fondest affection; and in a few weeks I healed up his wounds.

While tending him, I often noticed that he was revolving the events of the war in his mind, and that his whole thoughts were bent on undertaking new enterprises : for his character was of that stamp in which exertion amidst dangers and difficulties is preferred to idleness. Nor is he unprofitably employed who records worthy actions, which may animate others to imitate the virtues he attempts to describe.

CHAPTER X.

THE EXPEDITION TO CADIZ.

BEFORE Moore recovered from his wounds, his Majesty appointed him Colonel of the 52d regiment, a mark of the acceptance of his services in Holland. And he was hardly restored to health when he received an order from the Commander-in-Chief to proceed to Chelmsford, to take charge of, and discipline the troops assembled there.

Towards the end of this year Bonaparte escaped from Egypt, by that good fortune which so long attended him, and which beguiled him to imagine that his fate was superintended by a guardian star. The French nation, dazzled by the glory he had acquired in the field, submitted passively to his annihilating liberty, and usurping despotic power; although that was the false charge for which their innocent sovereign had been decapitated.

In war, the advantages of the supreme power of the state being wielded by the leader of the forces are very great. It was by this concentration of authorities, that ancient Rome, when in extremities, was often preserved. But in the British government there is the greatest division of power that perhaps was ever established in any country; for the naval and military commanders act independently of each other,—the one receiving orders from the Board of Admiralty, and the other from the Secretary of State; and these two authorities are subordinate to the Prime Minister, who is, in some degree, controlled by the opinions of the majority of the Cabinet. Lastly, Admirals, Generals, and Ministers, are all accountable to the King, responsible to the furious cabals in Parliament, and exposed to the libellous rage of the press. This confusion of control occasions mutability and dilatoriness in warlike operations; for the success of which, steadiness and celerity are essential.

The new French administration was quickly

organized, as despotic power is prompt; and on the 6th of May, 1800, Bonaparte set off for the conquest of Italy.

Early in spring, a scheme had been devised by Sir Charles Stuart, and approved of by the War Minister, to co-operate with the Austrians, who had nearly expelled the French from Italy. Fifteen thousand men were to embark from England; five thousand to be taken from the garrisons in the Mediterranean, and the whole to enter and occupy the maritime Alps. It was intended by this means to shut up the communication between France and Italy, and form a powerful diversion in favour of Austria; and it was also expected that the royalists in the South of France would be encouraged, by this force, to rise in revolt against Bonaparte.

Sir Charles applied to General Moore to accept a command in this expedition, which he willingly assented to. But unforeseen difficulties occurred, and intelligence was brought that a Spanish army, in alliance

with France, was about to invade Portugal.
The above project was then laid aside, fresh
instructions were given to Sir Charles Stuart,
who disapproved of them, and resigned his
command. In his stead Sir Ralph Abercrombie was appointed. The information
respecting Portugal proved false, and five
thousand of the troops who had been embarked, sailed for the Mediterranean. In
the middle of May, Sir Ralph, accompanied
by his friend Moore, followed in a frigate,
and arrived in six weeks at Minorca. But
previously Bonaparte scaled the Alps, and
burst into the Milanese, in the rear of the
Austrian forces. These were commanded by
Marshal Melas, who applied for a British
corps to strengthen the garrison of Genoa,
while he moved against the French. Accordingly, Sir Ralph Abercrombie embarked
four thousand men at Malta and Minorca,
(all that could be spared,) and sailed for
Genoa. But before he could reach his destination, the Austrian army was overthrown

at Marengo, their garrison at Genoa with-
drawn, and the neutrality of Tuscany
guaranteed. After these disasters, when
the French eagles approached the south,
the Queen of Naples took to flight, flut-
tering with her plumed King and the
affrighted courtiers into a British Admiral's
ship.

On learning this change of affairs, Sir
Ralph altered his course for Leghorn, to
which port the fleet had sailed. He went
on board the flag-ship to concert measures
with Lord Keith, the Admiral; and he had
also a conference with the Queen of Naples
and her Ministers. That vain and wanton
woman pressed him vehemently to undertake
the · defence of the Neapolitan dominions,
which he refused to do, his small force
being quite inadequate to contend with
the numerous French armies in Italy; and he
was well aware that no effective aid could
be expected from the Neapolitan soldiery,
who would be appalled by the sound, or even
by the sight of a cannon. He, however, of-

fered to garrison Messina, and defend Sicily, should the French attempt the conquest of that island. Nothing he could say made the slightest impression on that self-willed Queen. And as she persevered in urging Sir Ralph to yield to her opinion, he calmly replied, 'That without further orders from ' his Court, compliance was impossible.' Thus commenced a disagreement with the British Generals, which continued with augmenting animosity during the greater part of her reign.

Sir Ralph Abercrombie then sailed to Malta, which was closely blockaded by the British and Maltese; and Moore returned with the troops to Minorca, and commenced instructing them in their duty. Other regiments arrived successively from England, in a very defective state of discipline; consequently Moore, and all the officers, had abundant occupation to form them properly.

Despatches at length arrived from England, with positive orders respecting the employment of the forces; on which Sir Ralph embarked ten thousand men, and sailed back to Gibraltar, where he was joined by upwards of ten thousand more, under Sir James Pulteney. Storms, usual at the latter end of autumn, detained the fleet for some time at Tetuan Bay. But in an interval of moderate weather, the armament, consisting of one hundred and fifty ships, arrived off Cadiz, which was at that time infested with the plague.

The object of this combined expedition was to seize or destroy the Spanish fleet, and to burn the arsenal. On the 6th of October, General Moore and three thousand men were actually in boats to make the first landing; but before they rowed off, they were countermanded. The reasons for this, and for abandoning the design, are detailed in the following letter of the General to his father.

' Gibraltar Bay, 25th October, 1800.

' My dear Father,

* * * ' You must have heard of the ridiculous ' figure which we cut before Cadiz. I am

' sorry for Sir Ralph, because he will share
' the censure, though in justice none attaches
' to him.—His orders were to land and de-
' stroy the arsenal of Cadiz, if he was certain
' of bringing off the army. This certainty
' could only be had, in case the shipping, in
' which were our provisions and stores, could
' anchor in safety, so as to ensure to us, when
' landed, a constant communication with
' them. At Gibraltar, before we sailed, Lord
' Keith said this could be done, if, by pos-
' sessing the points of Rota and Fort Sta
' Catalina, we gave him the anchorage which
' lies between them. Upon this, the expe-
' dition was determined, and we accordingly
' sailed for Cadiz. When we got off that
' port, the naval officers best acquainted with
' the coast assured him, that there was no
' anchorage out of Cadiz Bay, which was safe
' from a south-west wind; that such might
' be expected at this late season, in which
' case the transports would certainly be
' blown on shore, and the ships of war be
' obliged to put to sea; and that as long as

' the wind was south-west, no communication
' whatever could be had between the fleet
' and the army on shore. Lord Keith was
' frightened at this opinion of his officers,
' and somewhat ashamed of what he had
' before asserted. He could not be got to
' adopt the opinion of his officers, nor totally
' to give up his own : though in my presence
' he was pushed by Sir Ralph to do so,
' who wished for a decided opinion from him
' one way or another ; that we might either
' immediately land, or return to Gibraltar.
' On the morning of the 6th inst., the signal
' was made to prepare to land. The fleet
' was then under weigh, at least ten miles
' from the shore. The flat-boats, however,
' agreeable to the signal, began to assemble
' round, the ships which contained the troops
' of the 1st division; viz., the brigade of
' Guards, and Reserve (the latter is my com-
' mand). It is not to be described, the bad
' arrangement and confusion which attended
' the assembling of the boats ; it was in-
' creased by the ships being under sail.

'About one o'clock in the afternoon, there
' were only three thousand men in boats,
' instead of five thousand, which the first
' division consisted of; and no more boats
' could be got; this, from want of arrange-
' ment. We were seven miles from the shore;
' before it would have been possible to land
' us, and return for more troops, it must have
' been dark. It was therefore evident, that
' the landing was to be effected with three
' thousand men, instead of five thousand;
' and these, instead of being immediately
' supported by a second division of five
' thousand, must trust to themselves for the
' night in an unknown country. Under
' these circumstances, Sir Ralph wisely de-
' termined to postpone the landing. He sent
' to Lord Keith to do so, and to desire that
' he would bring the fleet to an anchor, and
' make an arrangement to begin to land the
' troops next morning at daylight. We
' anchored accordingly that night, but in no
' order; and from everything I could observe,
' I was convinced that the same confusion

'which had attended the operations of the
' day, would attend those of the morning.

' In the course of the night, Lord Keith
' wrote to Sir Ralph, to state the danger of
' anchoring upon the coast; upon this, the
' expedition was given up, and orders were
' circulated in the night, to prepare to weigh
' in the morning. It began to blow from
' the south-west, which at any rate would
' have stopped the landing. It blew so hard,
' that had the first division landed the day
' before, it would probably have been cut off:
' it could neither have been re-embarked
' nor supported. Upon the whole, we have
' little to regret, for had we escaped every
' other misfortune, we must have caught the
' plague; which carries off daily many hun-
' dreds in Cadiz, and the neighbourhood.
' Sir Ralph, however, is much hurt: he feels
' the ridicule of doing nothing after making
' the display; this he was led into by Lord
' Keith, to whose bad management it was
' also owing, that we did not land on the 6th.

' Since we left Cadiz, we have been most

' unpleasantly situated, going between this
' place, Tetuan Bay, and the west coast of
' Africa. In none of them is there safe
' anchorage for a fleet, and we have been
' obliged to shift from the one to the other,
' according as the wind blew. Our com-
' manders have been waiting for orders,
' which are only now come.

' Before this reaches you, you will of
' course know that Sir James Pulteney goes
' with six battalions to Lisbon. The rest of
' the force, fifteen thousand, goes with Sir
' Ralph to Egypt. I belong to this last, and
' expect to sail for Minorca to-morrow. Sir
' Ralph and the last of the troops will not be
' away for several days. I know nothing of
' the policy which dictates this new service;
' I see many difficulties in the execution of
' it. I, however, have the greatest confidence
' in Sir Ralph's sagacity and judgment. Our
' army is not a bad one, and success against
' the French is more gratifying than against
' the miserable Spaniards. I once thought
' it probable I should see you this winter; of

'this there is now no chance, nor is there a
'possibility of saying when I am to have that
'pleasure. As these are not times for honour-
'able ease and retirement, I have no wish to
'be at home until the war is over. And it
'must be a consolation to my mother and
'you, that in following the course of my pro-
'fession, I am employed upon the service by
'much the most important that is going.

'My love to my Mother and Jane.

'Believe me ever, my dear Father,

'Most affectionately,

'JOHN MOORE.'

It appears certain, that had the boats
rowed to the shore, with Moore and the three
thousand soldiers, they must all have been
lost. Indeed, in war apparent mishaps are
often fortunate. Had the fleet which bore
Nicias and the flower of Athens to Syracuse,
been blown back by adverse winds to the
Piræus, they would have been mortified and
certainly scoffed at with Attic raillery : but
they would have escaped discomfiture,
slavery, and death.

Chapter XI.

THE CAMPAIGN IN EGYPT.

AFTER the fleet was driven from the anchorage off Cadiz, with the loss of some cables and anchors, it beat about the mouth of the Mediterranean, till fresh orders should arrive from England. And the soldiers cooped up in crowded transports were tossed about in that tempestuous season in a comfortless and perilous condition. Despatches with decisive orders arrived at last, directing five thousand men to be landed in Portugal, for the defence of that kingdom, and the remainder of the army to proceed up the Straits of Gibraltar to be employed in the invasion of Egypt. To retain that conquest had been a favourite object of Bonaparte; who, at great risk, had sent vessels there with supplies of arms and stores of all kinds wanted; most of which had escaped the vigilance of the British cruisers. But intercepted letters from the French officers, filled with complaints and disgust at the country, raised expectations that the army was much reduced : these, together with the danger which menaced India from that quarter, prompted the British government to resolve to restore the country, if possible, to the Turks. It was believed, from the best intelligence that had been procured, that the French forces then remaining in Egypt did not exceed thirteen or fourteen thousand men : whereas, it was afterwards found that they exceeded thirty-two thousand infantry and cavalry, and were furnished with above a thousand pieces of artillery.* The whole force which Sir Ralph Abercrombie was enabled to muster for this undertaking, exclusive of the sick, did not amount to fifteen thousand soldiers. Had the French strength been known, the project would never have been attempted; it was proceeded on from misinformation.

It was in the latter end of the autumn, that

---

* ' History of the British Expedition to Egypt,' by Sir Robert Wilson.—pp. 255, 256.

Major-General Moore sailed with the first division of the troops for Minorca, and after a short stay, passed on to Malta; his sentiments on entering upon this daring enterprise, appear in a letter to his mother.

'Malta, December 18th, 1800.

' My dear Mother,

    ' I wrote to my father some days ago,
' expecting then to sail immediately. We
' have been detained by contrary winds; the
' wind now is fair; the signal for all persons
' belonging to the first division to repair on
' board, is this instant made. If they get
' off this afternoon, we of the second division
' will certainly follow to-morrow.

    ' I received your letter of the 2nd October,
' at Gibraltar. There is but a distant pros-
' pect of my making one of your Richmond
' parties; the business we are now going
' upon, must occupy us until midsummer;
' and then, if the war continues, some other
' work will be found for us. My mind is
' so much made up upon this subject, that

' I hardly wish to return until there is peace.
' I hope then to. meet Graham, and to pass
' some years .comfortably with you, in the
' neighbourhood of Marsh Gate*. We do
' not consider this Egyptian expedition in
' the melancholy light that you do at home.
' The army, I think, rather like it. I,
' in particular, prefer it to anything that
' has yet offered. I am persuaded of the
' necessity of driving the French from Egypt,
' before we can make peace. Sir Ralph
' is quite keen about it, and is ten years
' younger since he left England. We are all
' healthy, and there is a greater chance of our
' continuing so, as the men get daily more
' accustomed to the climate, and habituated to
' the diet on board ship. I was tired of the
' sailing in the Mediterranean, whilst there
' seemed to be no determined object; so that we
' were roving in quest of adventures, and the
' chapter of accidents. But now that tedium
' is over, the mind is fully occupied with the
' ultimate object ; and the stoppage here, and

* Near Richmond, where Dr. Moore lived.

' in Greece, countries quite new to us, breaks
' in upon the sameness of a sea voyage, and
' prevents its being tiresome. . . .

  ' Farewell, and believe me,

    ' My dear Mother,

   ' Your's ever affectionately,

       ' J. M.'

Before the whole of the troops arrived,
Sir Ralph had many confidential, serious consultations with Moore respecting the plan of
the campaign ; and whether it would be preferable to attempt landing near Alexandria
to besiege it ; or in the vicinity of Damietta,
and sail up that branch of the Nile to attack
Grand Cairo. All the information he could
procure respecting the coast, the harbours,
roads, and winds, were well weighed by this
very able and most considerate General.
But the more the business was examined
into, the more difficulties were discovered;
and it began to be suspected, that the French
army was more numerous than had been reported. But Sir Ralph, steady to his determination, sailed to Marmorice Bay, the

rendezvous for the armament. As it was of great importance to ascertain what aid might be expected from the Turkish government, he deputed Moore with instructions to the Grand Vizir, who was lying with an army near Jaffa. A war-brig was appointed to convey him to the Turkish camp, and the account of the negotiation shall be given in his own words.

' * I landed at Jaffa on the 9th of January;
' the first thing I heard, was the death of
' Brigadier-General Koehler, who died of a
' putrid fever, on the 29th December, after
' three days' illness. I immediately pro-
' ceeded to the Vizir's camp, which was
' about a mile from the town, and I com-
' municated to Major Holloway, the senior
' British officer since poor Koehler's death,
' the object of my mission. He took me first
' to the Reis Effendi, and then to the
' Vizir; their tents are very fine; they were
' seated cross-legged on sofas, with numerous

* MS. Journal.

' attendants standing on each side. We
' were presented with pipes, then coffee, and
' then chocolate; each of which are stages of
' compliment, which are served out according
' to the rank of the visitor, or the respect they
' wish to show him. The Reis Effendi was
' four years secretary to the embassy in
' England, and he speaks French, which is
' uncommon for a Turk. The conversation
' generally is carried on by means of a Drog-
' man, or interpreter. The first visit was con-
' fined to compliment; an hour was fixed in
' the evening for business. I had expressed
' to the Reis Effendi, that my business was of
' a nature not to be trusted to the common
' interpreter; I found in the evening, with
' the Vizir, only two persons, the Reis
' Effendi and Kaia Beg, the former of whom
' interpreted. I stayed with them near three
' hours, and had an opportunity to explain
' fully the plan proposed by Sir Ralph, and
' everything contained in my instructions.
' They talked a great deal in Turkish; the
' Vizir made a few objections, not very

' portant, which I answered; upon the whole,
' he seemed much pleased, and said he should
' be happy that the operations should com-
' mence soon.

' I wrote next morning the heads of a
' plan, such as I thought met the Vizir's
' wishes, without deviating from the spirit of
' Sir Ralph's instructions. I carried it to the
' Reis Effendi, and begged he would show it
' to the Vizir: if he approved of it, I should
' draw it out for his Highness and me to sign.
' It was agreed that I should return in the
' evening. When I did so, he told me the
' Vizir was indisposed and could not see me,
' but he would send to me in the course of
' next day. In the mean time I lived with
' Major Holloway and the British officers of
' the mission. A very good tent was found
' me, and a dinner from the Vizir's kitchen
' every day. I employed myself in observing
' the Turkish camp, their soldiery, and man-
' ners, so different from everything I had
' seen before. The death of General Koehler
' was particularly unfortunate at this time, as

' he certainly knew something of the state
' of the magazines, the administration of the
' Turkish army, and its organization. Major
' Holloway did not; and as I could not alto-
' gether depend upon what either the Reis
' Effendi or Vizir asserted in conversation on
' these subjects, I applied in writing to the
' Vizir for information, both with respect to
' the effective force under his command, the
' extent of his magazines, the means he had
' of forwarding them as the army advanced,
' and the measures he had taken to keep
' them complete. I applied also, in the
' same manner, for the information he had
' received respecting the intentions of the
' enemy. In a conference I had with the
' Vizir in consequence of this application, he
' told me that at Jaffa and El Alrich he had
' sufficient supplies of ammunition and bis-
' cuit for his army; but that he had no barley
' for the cavalry or beasts of the army; with-
' out which it would be impossible for him to
' pass the desert; and that he had long ago
' taken steps to provide a sufficient quantity,

' and was looking hourly for the arrival of
' the ships that were to bring it. He stated
' his force at seven thousand five hundred
' cavalry, and the same number of infantry,
' with fifty pieces of field-artillery. I de-
' sired that he might send me in writing
' these answers to my letter.

' By the Vizir's confession, the advance of
' his army depended on the arrival of barley.
' But, upon further enquiry, I had every rea-
' son to believe that the quantity even of
' biscuit was by no means sufficient to
' enable his army to act, if he was detained
' any time upon the frontier of Egypt. From
' a view of his troops, and from everything I
' could learn or observe of their composition
' and discipline, I could not think they were
' other than a wild, ungovernable mob, in-
' capable of being directed to any useful pur-
' pose. And as they were destitute of every-
' thing that is required in an army, and their
' chief, the Vizir, was a weak-minded old man,
' without talent, or any military knowledge,
' it was in vain to expect any co-operation

T 2

' from them. At any rate, the prospect of
' assistance from them was not sufficient to
' make it advisable to change any plan,
' merely upon their account, which in other
' respects might be preferred. This is the
' opinion I formed, and which I gave to Sir
' Ralph upon my return. The Vizir, how-
' ever, signed the plan I at first proposed,
' after detaining me five days for that, and
' for the answers to the different questions I
' have mentioned.

  ' I got from him little or no information
' respecting the French in Egypt; for though
' the communication from Cairo is open, and
' persons are frequently coming from thence,
' they bring no information: they seem
' equally ignorant of its importance, and of
' the means of obtaining it.

  ' The plague is always in their camp; it
' rages with sometimes more, sometimes less
' violence; a great many persons died of it
' when I was there. The Vizir's family, in
' particular, were very sickly, nine of them
' were buried in one day, and the loss in the

' camp was estimated one day at two hun-
' dred persons.

' The Turks are so extremely careless, that
' the clothes of the persons who die of the
' plague are sold publicly at auction ; and
' are generally worn by those who buy them,
' without ever being washed.

' Their army has lost six thousand persons
' by the plague, within these seven months.

' Upon taking leave of the Vizir, it is cus-
' tomary to receive the present of a pelisse,
' which he throws over your shoulders. It is
' not proper to refuse this present ; but I re-
' quested it might be sent to me, not wishing
' to run the risk of catching the plague by
' wearing it before it was fumigated. The
' Vizir's army is not composed of profes-
' sional soldiers, the Janissaries are the only
' troops they have of that description. Even
' these being generally residents in the same
' districts, and, having no parades or exer-
' cises, follow trades and other occupations.
' The Bashaws of the districts through which
' the Vizir passes are ordered to attend him,

' each with a certain number of followers.
' These are the inhabitants of the country,
' who have all arms of their own, and attend
' on foot or horseback according to their
' means.

' They are, in general, a stout, active, and
' hardy people; and are allowed to be indivi-
' dually brave. There are certainly mate-
' rials of which excellent soldiers might be
' formed; but under a Turkish government
' everything becomes debased.'

Sir Ralph had been prepared for the unfavourable report made to him by Moore on
his return: and both were convinced that, in
their first operations at least, no reliance
could be put on any assistance from the
Turks. Notwithstanding which, Sir Ralph
resolved to land on the coast near Alexandria, and if possible besiege that town. A
council of war of Admirals and Generals
was called, to whom Sir Ralph explained his
intentions. The place of landing and every
detail was there discussed, and fixed upon.

And as he had not forgot the confusion that had been experienced at Cadiz, he practised disembarkations on the shore, until both the soldiers and sailors became expert at the business. The preparations were pressed forward; but Turkish sloth is unconquerable. Yet some horses, though of a bad quality, were procured for the field-artillery, and to mount about four hundred dragoons; still near six hundred others were wanted. A few mules also were obtained for drawing stores. But to counterbalance these acquisitions, our cruizers were blown off the coast by a storm, and two large French frigates slipped into Alexandria, conveying eight hundred soldiers, and warlike stores; and warning was thus given of the meditated attack. It also happened, that a polacre from Alexandria was captured, on board of which was Tallien, the celebrated revolutionist. He, and his attendants, being hostile to the present French government, gave information of the real number of the French army; but this intelligence was not credited.

for it was naturally imagined to be a monstrous exaggeration to deter our Generals from landing.

When all things were prepared, violent and contrary winds prevailed. As soon, however, as the weather permitted, the fleet put to sea, and reached Aboukir Bay.

Sir Ralph, accompanied by Moore, then got into a cutter, and rowed towards the beach, to reconnoitre the coast. They observed the French at work on a height, and at other places; and although the ground was most favourable for defence, yet as no time was to be lost, orders were issued for the landing to take place next morning at daybreak. But a high wind arose that night, which rendered it impracticable. The weather did not moderate until after five days; when Moore was despatched to reconnoitre again, and to discover what additional works might in the interval have been constructed. He was rowed to a bomb vessel, which lay at anchor within a mile and a half of the shore. The land rises from the beach with inequalities : on the left there were groves of palm trees, and on the right, a steep sandy hill, within reach of the guns of the fort of Aboukir, which is situated on the shore ; but the enemy's works were all masked and invisible. He, however, knew of their existence, and clearly perceived that the enemy would be completely covered from the fire of gunboats, or of any vessels from the sea ; while the beach was exposed to be swept by cannon and musketry from the heights. Notwithstanding the strength of the enemy's position, the determination to land was persevered in.

Early in the morning (March 10th) the reserve, commanded by Moore ; the Guards, and another brigade, commanded by Generals Ludlow and Cootes, were embarked in boats ; this, the first division, amounted to five thousand, five hundred men. Before the signal was made to advance, General Hope was despatched by Sir Ralph to Moore, to ask, ' *Whether he continued of the same mind, to

* Journal, MS.

‘ land exactly opposite to the hill, or if it
‘ would not be better to incline more to the
‘ right, as the hill appeared to be very steep
‘ in front.’ Moore answered, ‘ the steepness
‘ is not such as can prevent our ascending,
‘ and is therefore rather favourable.’ General Hope then told him, that Sir Ralph,
who was with Lord Keith in the nearest
bomb vessel, desired him to say, that ‘ if
‘ the fire from the enemy was so great that
‘ the men could not bear it, he would make
‘ the signal to retire ; and therefore desired
‘ that Moore and Cochrane should look
‘ occasionally to the ship in which Sir
‘ Ralph was.’ The humane feelings of Abercrombie, when ordering his soldiers on this
most desperate duty, burst out in this final
injunction.

For two hours the French had been spec-
tators of the preparations, and were seen
drawn up on the heights, with their cannon
ready pointed. The signal to proceed being
given, some gun vessels and armed launches
were sent forward, to clear the beach. Ge-

neral Moore, and his staff*, embarked in
the boat of Captain Cochrane, the naval commander of the disembarkation, which, to direct all the movements, advanced ahead of the
line of boats containing the troops. These
followed in perfect order, the soldiers sitting
on the benches, close together, with unloaded
arms, as Moore had commanded. When
the boats came within range of the enemy's
batteries, fifteen pieces of ordnance from the
opposite hill, and the artillery of the Castle
of Aboukir, opened upon them, with round
and grape shot; and on advancing farther,
musket-balls were also showered down. The
British soldiers huzzaed occasionally, but
returned not a shot. Numbers of them were
killed and wounded, some boats were sunk,
and the nearest were turned aside to save
the drowning men, while the remainder
were rowed steadily onward. Sir Ralph
Abercrombie stood on the deck of a ship,

---

* The officers who accompanied General Moore in this boat
rose afterwards to high rank in the service: they were Sir Alex-
ander Cochrane, Sir Hildebrand Oakes, Sir George Murray,
Aide-de-camp Anderson, and Brigade-Major Groves.

looking forward with intense anxiety; and
saw with horror the storm of iron and leaden
balls descending upon his soldiers. He held
in his hand the signal for retreat, and hardly
refrained from raising it. Captain Cochrane's boat first reached the strand, and the
officers all stepped out. The boats with the
troops then grounded, and Moore instantly
drew them up in line, and gave the word to
load.

He mounted the hill at their head, reached
the summit, fired a volley, charged the enemy, drove them down the hill, and captured
four cannon. Then he stopped the pursuit,
as he heard a heavy fire on his left: for
General Oakes, when bringing up the remainder of the reserve, met with a sharp
resistance from the enemy's infantry and
cavalry; yet he gallantly repulsed both, and
joined Moore. Towards the left, the Guards,
on quitting the boats, and before they
formed, were furiously attacked by the French
horse, and thrown into disorder; but they
repelled the enemy, and advanced to their

station on the left of the reserve. The enemy then fell back on all sides; but the want of cavalry prevented any further pursuit.

The French troops were a portion of Bonaparte's far-famed Italian army; who had looked down exultingly on boats filled with troops approaching their batteries, being quite confident of easily overpowering them: but when driven from their lofty station, and forced to leave their cannon behind them, they were confounded. Yet the victors sustained a heavy loss, especially while exposed, on the sea, to unrequited carnage: the reserve especially, which landed first, and stormed the hill, suffered severely.

In the evening the rest of the army landed, marched forward a few miles, and took post on a sandy plain. The next day was consumed in digging for water, which was found; and in landing, and dragging through the sand, artillery, ammunition, and provisions. These laborious duties were chiefly performed by men; as the vessels which contained the mules, and many of the horses, were wrecked at sea. This was a very grievous loss, as there were few horses even for the artillery,—in both of which the French abounded. Most of the dragoons remained dismounted, others were. badly mounted, and so few in number that they could never be opposed to the numerous cavalry of the enemy, which hovered on the front and flanks of the army.

A small detachment was sent to besiege the Castle of Aboukir in the rear ; and Moore was directed to advance and take a more advantageous position, on a narrower part of the isthmus, between the sea and the Lake Maadie.

As he moved forward some brisk skirmishing occurred with his light troops and the enemy's cavalry, who retired before them. He took possession of the ground intended, and the enemy withdrew, only leaving patroles and videttes in his front. Sir Ralph, with the other columns, then moved up and formed in the rear. Rapid movements were prevented, by the impossibility of getting quickly forward the necessary stores.

On the 12th of March, the army advanced in two columns, the reserve forming the vanguard of each, led· by Generals Moore and Oakes. They soon fell in with the enemy's cavalry, which commenced skirmishing, but retired as the columns advanced. On reaching a tower, named Mandara, Moore mounted up to reconnoitre, and saw a large body of infantry approaching. On giving notice of which Sir Ralph ordered a line to be formed, which was executed in perfect order in the face of the enemy. They halted, and seeing the resistance they were likely to encounter, retreated; and the British took up a more advanced position, close to that of the French. Moore then received orders to take the command of the advanced posts, and two fresh additional regiments were sent to him, as the reserve were exceedingly fatigued by their previous exertions. With these he covered the front of the army with a chain of posts, communicating with each other, and regularly relieved, and all were kept on the alert, ready for action.

The enemy, who received some reinforcements from Grand Cairo, took possession of a swelling ridge of hills, defended by numerous artillery, and flanked by six hundred cavalry. Their infantry amounted to about five thousand four hundred. Sir Ralph disposed his troops into three columns, in order to attack them, and to compel them to retire into Alexandria. The left column, under General Hutchinson, was to commence the action, and to endeavour to turn the enemy's right. The centre column, commanded by General Craddock, was directed to move in unison, and the reserve covered the right flank.

At six in the morning the army advanced in the above order; and the enemy moved forward to meet them with a numerous artillery: they commenced a heavy fire of cannon and musketry on the left and central columns, which were also charged by cavalry. The cavalry, unable to penetrate the ranks, were repelled by a shower of balls ; the line was formed, and the action became general. The French were forced back, but retired fighting, and disputed every favourable elevation of the ground. The reserve advanced rapidly in column, guarding the right flank, but exposed to a heavy cannonade from the front, and to musketry from light infantry and hussars on the flank. Though the destruction was great, order was preserved. The whole army pressed forward, and gained the heights on which the French had been originally posted, who retreated across the plain in great confusion. Had there been a good body of horse to fall upon the fugitives, the whole artillery, and most of the infantry, must have been cut off. But this finishing power was wanting, and the enemy were enabled to escape to strong fortified heights in front of Alexandria.

Sir Ralph then met Moore, and a consultation was held *. ' It was determined that ' General Hutchinson, with some brigades

---

* The Journal, MS.

' which had been least engaged, should at-
' tack the enemy's right, and that the re-
' serve, supported by the Guards, should
' attack their left, near the sea. As General
' Hutchinson had a considerable circuit to
' make, Moore's attack was to be regulated by
' the other. But when Hutchinson got round
' to the left, opposite to the ground intended
' to be attacked, he perceived that the
' enemy's position was very strong, defended
' by a numerous artillery, and commanded
' by the guns of the fortified hills near Alex-
' andria. He therefore halted, and sent to
' inform Sir Ralph that the heights could
' not be carried without a considerable loss,
' and if carried, as they would be exposed to
' the fire of the fortified hills, it would be
' impossible to maintain them without en-
' trenching themselves, for which they had
' not the means.'

General Hope was first sent, then Sir
Ralph himself rode to the spot to reconnoitre;
and after some consideration, the attack was
fortunately given up, and the army marched

back to the camp which the French had previously occupied.

To deliberate during action, and to alter a design commenced, was a hard necessity, occasioned by the impossibility of obtaining previous intelligence of the French defences. Until Sir Ralph saw them, he knew them not; and as his cannon could not be dragged through the sand as fast as the army advanced, his soldiers were swept down by artillery, without his having the means of retaliating.

Two victories had now been won, but only fourteen miles of a sandy beach gained, while the army was reduced in numbers, and obliged to halt till provisions and the warlike apparatus were brought from the fleet to the camp. Among other distresses, fuel could hardly be procured to dress the food. No aid was yet sent them by the Turkish government, on whose territories, and in whose behoof they were fighting; and although a detachment had been ordered from India, no co-operation from so distant a region could be looked for; and the intelligence of the paucity of the French in Egypt, upon which the expedition had been planned by the British cabinet, was now ascertained to be fallacious.

On the 20th March Sir Ralph visited Moore, and laid open to him his most inward thoughts. His mind was troubled with the difficulties he had to encounter, but he resolved to persevere with dauntless resolution, and concluded by saying *, ' That as soon as the heavy cannon were got up, and entrenching tools ' forwarded, he thought it incumbent on them ' to make an effort. His plan was to endeavour in the night to push forward the artillery, and form the troops under such cover ' as he could find; and at daylight advance ' to the attack of both the enemy's flanks. ' If they failed they could still return to their ' present position, and maintain it until ' another could be prepared in the rear to ' favour a retreat, and finally, their re-em-

* The Journal.

' barkation. He regretted the throwing away
' so fine an army; and added that he believed
' nobody could envy him in his situation.'

This plan would soon have been put in
execution, if the French had continued on
the defensive in their strong entrenchments.
But Menou, their commander, came down
with a reinforcement from Grand Cairo to
Alexandria; and reproached his generals for
suffering the British to exist so long in Egypt
where he commanded. Then with over-
weening arrogance, he resolved to march
down from the fortified heights and overthrow
them in the plain. The British were encamped in two lines, about four miles from
Alexandria. The right wing, formed of the
reserve, was most advanced, and a small
redoubt was thrown up in front; the ruins
of the ancient Nicopolis were behind, towards the sea. Troops were posted in both,
and the remainder of the reserve were placed
on the left of these. The centre, and the
left wing of the army, were in some degree
refused, being inclined obliquely towards the

extremity of the Lake Maadie, where some gun-boats lay to protect that flank. The space from that lake to the sea, above a mile and a half in extent, was thus occupied.

Menou, observing the forward position of the British right wing, resolved with his greatest force to attack it, and the centre; and to make a false attack on the left wing. After defeating and turning the right, his whole army was ordered to rush on and drive the British into the Lake Maadie. The accomplishment of these imperious orders will now be related in General Moore's own words.

On the 20th of March,* ' I was the general ' of the day, and after visiting all the ad- ' vanced posts, remained with the left picket ' of the reserve until four in the morning of ' the 21st. The enemy had been perfectly ' quiet during the night, nothing had been ' observed from them but some rockets, which ' it was not uncommon for them to throw up.

* Journal.

' Conceiving everything quiet, I left orders
' with the field-officer to retire his posts at
' daylight, and I rode towards the left, to
' give similar orders to the other pickets as
' I went along. When I reached the picket
' of the guards, I heard a fire of musketry on
' the left, but everything continuing quiet on
' the right, and from the style of the firing,
' I suspected it was a false alarm. * * * *
' I was trotting towards the left, when a firing
' commenced from the pickets of the reserve;
' I immediately turned to my aid-de-camp,
' Captain Sewell, and said, " This is the real
' " attack; let us gallop to the redoubt." I
' met, as I returned, all the pickets falling
' back, and by the time I reached the re-
' doubt, in which the 28th regiment was
' posted, I found it warmly attacked. The
' day was not yet broken, and the dark-
' ness was made greater by the smoke of the
' guns and small arms. My arrangement in
' case of attack had been made beforehand.
' I had agreed with General Oakes, that the
' redoubt, and the old ruin in front of the

' right of the army, in which I had posted
' the 28th and 58th regiments, must be sup-
' ported, and was the ground for the reserve
' to fight upon. In fact, if those posts were
' carried by the enemy, it would have been
' impossible for our army to remain in their
' position. The general orders were for the
' troops to stand to their arms an hour before
' daylight, and fortunately they had fallen in
' before the attack commenced. Colonel
' Paget*, with the 28th, manned the redoubt,
' and had two companies in reserve, which he
' formed on the left of it, as the redoubt was
' open in the rear.

' The 58th regiment lined the old ruins
' which were retired twenty.or thirty yards
' behind the right flank of the redoubt, and
' swept the ground between it and the sea.
' Agreeable to what had been concerted,
' General Oakes, upon the attack com-
' mencing, brought down the left wing of the
' 42nd (Highlanders) to the left, and I sent

* Afterwards General Sir Edward Paget.

' Captain Anderson for the right wing, with
' orders to the 23rd regiment, and four flank
' companies of the 40th, to support the ruins.
' We could feel the effect of · the enemy's
' fire, but it was impossible as yet to see
' what he was about; his drums were beating
' the charge, and they were with their voices
' encouraging one another to advance. My
' horse was shot in the face, and became so
' unmanageable, that I was obliged to dis-
' mount. Colonel Paget, whilst I was speak-
' ing to him on the platform of the redoubt,
' received a shot in the neck which knocked
' him down. He said he was killed, and I
' thought so; he, however, recovered a little,
' and was put upon his horse.

    ' About this time, the left wing of the 42nd
' arrived on the left. Some person told me
' at that moment, that a column of French
' had turned our left. I thought that in the
' dark they had mistaken the 42nd for the
' French, and said so. I could distinguish
' them forming exactly where I had ordered
' them. But Colonel Paget, who had not yet

' retired, rode up to me, and said, " I assure
' " you, that the French have turned us, and
' " are moving towards the ruins." I looked
' to where he pointed, and accordingly saw
' a battalion of French in column, completely
' in our rear. The right wing of the 42nd
' arrived at this instant; I ran to them,
' ordered them to face to the right about, and
' shewed them the French completely in their
' power. They drove them into the ruins, and
' not a man of these French escaped being
' killed, wounded, or taken. The instant this
' was done, I led the regiment back to the
' flank of the redoubt; we met another
' column of the French, which had also pene-
' trated. We attacked them, and I received
' a shot in my leg. At this time, I met Sir
' Ralph, and told him what had passed at
' the ruins. The 42nd, and part of the 28th,
' drove this other column, but pursuing too
' far, got into disorder, and were attacked
' suddenly by cavalry. I had difficulty, from
' the wound in my leg, in walking, and Major
' Honeyman lent me his horse. The French

' cavalry were completely amongst us, but our
' men, though in disorder, rallied, and brought
' down with their fire so many men and
' horses, that the rest were glad to get off.
' The great object of the French was to gain
' the redoubt: ours to defend it. We could
' now see pretty well about us.

' They made another effort with a line of
' infantry to attack the redoubt in front and
' on both flanks. The 58th regiment, in the
' ruins, allowed them to approach within sixty
' yards, and then gave their fire so effectually
' as to knock down a great number of them;
' the rest went off. Upon the left, the 42nd
' and 28th repulsed what was in their front,
' but were again charged by a large body of
' cavalry, who penetrated, got into the re-
' doubt, and behind us. Sir Ralph was ac-
' tually taken by a French dragoon, but a
' soldier of the 42nd shot the man. I was
' obliged to put spurs to my horse to get
' clear, and I galloped to the ruins, to bring
' up some of the troops from thence, which I
' knew were formed, and in good order. The

' 28th regiment, who were lining the parapet
' of the redoubt, without quitting their posts,
' turned round, and killed the dragoons who
' had penetrated there. The 42nd regiment;
' though broken, were individually fighting;
' and I ordered the flank companies of the
' 40th from the ruins, to pour in a couple of
' vollies, though at the risk of hurting some
' of our own people. The field was instantly
' covered with men and horses; horses gal-
' loping without riders; in short, the cavalry
' were destroyed. , Every attack the French
' had made had been repulsed with slaughter.
' In the dark some confusion was unavoid-
' able; but our men, whenever the French ap-
' peared, had gone boldly up to them. Even
' the cavalry breaking in had not dismayed
' them. As the day broke, the foreign bri-
' gade, under Brigadier-General Stuart, came
' from the second line to our support; shared
' in the latter part of the action, and behaved
' with spirit. Our cartridges were expended,
' and our guns for want of ammunition had
' not fired for some time. Daylight enabled

' us to get our men into order, and as the
' enemy's artillery was galling us, I got as
' many men under the cover of the redoubt
' as I could. We were for an hour without a
' cartridge. The enemy during the time
' were pounding us with shot and shells, and
' distant musketry. Our artillery could not
' return a shot, and had their infantry again
' advanced, we must have repelled them with
' the bayonet. Our fellows would have done
' it, I never saw men more determined
' to do their duty; but the French had suf-
' fered so severely, that they could not get
' their men to make another attempt. They
' continued in our front, until ammuni-
' tion for our guns was brought up. They
' then very soon retreated. The great effort
' of the French was against our right, oppo-
' site to the reserve; another column had
' also attacked the Guards, who were upon
' the left of the reserve, it was repulsed with
' loss. The rest of the army was not en-
' gaged. Letters were found from Menou to

' a general officer, by which it appears that
' the whole (disposable) French force in
' Egypt had been concentrated for this
' attack. Menou, as well as all his army,
' had been quite confident of success. The
' prisoners say, their numbers were from
' twelve to fourteen thousand. They add,
' that they had never been fought till now;
' that the actions in Italy were nothing com-
' pared to those they have fought since we
' landed. Our loss is not yet ascertained; I
' hope it will not be found to exceed seven or
' eight hundred; that of the French must be,
' I think, from two to three thousand. I
' never saw a field so strewed with dead.
' Our effective force was not more than ten
' thousand. Sir Ralph received a shot in the
' thigh, but remained in the field, until the
' action was over, and was then conveyed to
' the Foudroyant. Amongst the last shots
' which were fired, a ball killed the horse
' Major Honeyman had lent me. The wound
' in my leg, which I received in the be-

' ginning of the action, had become painful
' and stiff towards nine o'clock when the
' affair ended.

' General Oakes was also wounded about
' the same time, and nearly in the same part
' of the leg that I was; but we had both been
' able to continue to do our duty.'

Some more particulars written subsequently, respecting the heroic Abercrombie,
shall not be omitted.

' Sir Ralph had always been accused of
' exposing his person too much; I never
' knew him carry this so far as in this action.
' When it was so dark that I could scarcely
' distinguish, I saw him close in the rear of
' the 42nd regiment, without any of his
' family. He was afterwards joined by Ge-
' neral Hope. When the French cavalry
' charged us the second time, and our men
' were disordered, I called and waved with my
' hand to him to retire, but he was instantly
' surrounded by the hussars. He received a
' cut from a sabre in the breast, which
' pierced through his clothes, but only grazed

' the flesh. He must have been taken or
' killed, if a soldier had not shot the hus-
' sar.'

Either before or after this encounter, Sir
Ralph received a shot in the thigh which
he concealed, and remained on the field till
the battle was won; then growing faint from
loss of blood, he was conveyed on board Lord
Keith's ship. Moore being taken into another ship, on account of his own wound, never
again saw his friend, who in a few days ex-
pired. On the day following this mournful
event, Moore, when suffering from grief and
pain, wrote in his journal as follows :—

' Sir Ralph was a truly upright, honour-
' able, and judicious man; his great sagacity,
' which had been pointed all his life to mi-
' litary matters, made him an excellent
' officer. The disadvantage he laboured
' under was being extremely short-sighted.
' He, therefore, stood in need of good execu-
' tive Generals under him. It was impos-
' sible, knowing him as I did, not to have
' the greatest respect and friendship for him.

' He had ever treated me with marked kind-
' ness. The only consolation I feel is, that
' his death has been nearly that which he
' himself wished ; and his country, grateful to
' his memory, will hand down his name to
' posterity with the admiration it deserves.'

In this action near thirteen hundred
British were killed and wounded. The
French lost four thousand ; but had Sir
Ralph been furnished with a due proportion
of cannon, and a corps of cavalry to fall
upon the fugitives, few of the whole army
would have escaped to Alexandria. Captain
Anderson, General Moore's brave aide-de-
camp, was environed in the second charge
of the French hussars, and severely wounded:
the General, also, had nearly fallen into their
hands, and the ball which pierced his leg
endangered the loss of the limb ; but this
fortunately was averted by severe operations.
He was long confined, and reduced to a very
feeble state ; yet in the month of May he was
so far restored as to be able to use crutches,
and was removed in a boat to Rosetta, on

the banks of the Nile, for better air.   During
this tedious confinement, he could only assist
the public affairs by his counsel.   How different is this course of life from that of soft
voluptuaries,—ever searching for, or chasing
pleasure, too fleet to be caught, or too nimble
to be held; and who prefers following those
who neglect her allurements and pursue the
perilous tracks of glory!

The command of the army devolved on
General Hutchinson, and the French retired
to their entrenched position in front of Alexandria.   The British were too inferior in
number, even after their successes, to attempt
the siege of that city, which could receive
reinforcements from Cairo.   Yet the consequences of the three victories were most important.   Multitudes of Arabs, witnesses of
the last battle, had testified their admiration
of British valour, and joy at the flight of
the French, whom they abhorred for their
cruelty and rapacity.   They brought into
the camp vegetables and fresh provisions
in abundance, for which they were justly

recompensed; and these refreshments were a great relief to the soldiers. And, what was of still more consequence, in a few days a Turkish fleet anchored in Aboukir Bay, from which the Captain Pacha landed with between five and six thousand Turks.

The good news, likewise, soon reached the Grand Vizir's camp, who was lingering at El-Arish. Great rejoicings were made, and in a few days one division of his army was sent forward, crossed the desert, and reached Catieh, in Egypt, without opposition. The two remaining divisions followed.

General Hutchinson's first occupation was to strengthen the lines across the isthmus, to secure the camp against any attack from the garrison of Alexandria. He next detached Colonel Spencer to attack Rosetta on the western branch of the Nile, with twelve hundred British; who were accompanied by above four thousand of the Turks who had lately arrived.

At their approach the French evacuated the town, which Spencer took possession of.

He then advanced, while the enemy skirmished and retreated before him. At El Hamet, situated higher up the Nile, he halted, and a reinforcement was sent him there; on which he detached Lord Dalhousie to lay siege to St. Julien, a strong fort commanding the mouth of one branch of the river. The Captain Pacha chose to be present at this siege, and displayed, on the principal battery, great personal bravery, and fired regularly one of the cannon himself. When the walls were breached, the fort capitulated.

About this time, intelligence was received that the Vizir was crossing the desert, and also an intimation was sent, that a corps from India might soon be expected at Suez. It therefore became requisite for co-operation, and for the security of this Indian reinforcement, that General Hutchinson should move into the Delta. But as it was an important object to preserve the lines before Alexandria, he took great care to fortify them well; and acceded reluctantly to another measure, which was strongly urged by both

the naval and military officers, yet quite re-
pugnant to the opinion of General Moore.
The neck of land separating the Lake Maadie
from the Lake Mareotis was cut through;
by which the canal conveying fresh water
from the Nile to Alexandria was destroyed,
and the Mareotis was filled with salt water.
To what distance the sea might flow by this
opening, and what devastation might be produced, could not then be ascertained. The
Lake Mareotis* was an excavation made in a
desert, of prodigious extent, and great depth,
begun in a very early age, by King Moeris,
and finished by his successors. It was a
work of the greatest utility, formed to receive
the waters of the Nile when the inundations
were superabundant; and to be an ample
reservoir when they were [deficient. Two
pyramids were erected in the Lake, and the
portentous labyrinth on its bank. These
have long been consumed by time; and now

* Vide Herodot., Plin., Rolin, Moreri, &c. &c.—There are
however some antiquarians who doubt if this is the site of the
ancient Lake Mareotis, as well as the other facts.

the lake itself is sea. All lovers of antiquity will lament that, for the protection of the side of a small camp, one of the most stupendous works that was ever executed by man has been irreparably destroyed.

Successive detachments were sent off to the encampment at El Hamet, and at length General Hutchinson proceeded there himself, leaving General Coote to maintain the lines before Alexandria, with six thousand five hundred men.

The French had collected a considerable force at Ramanieh, a town situated on the Nile; this they fortified strongly; and assembled a number of armed vessels and gunboats, to put a stop to all farther advancement. General Hutchinson made preparations to dislodge them; and moved on with about four thousand British, and as many Turks, expecting great resistance. But the French had now lost their eagerness for combat; for their light troops and cavalry made only the kind of opposition requisite to secure a retreat. The entrenched town of

Ramanieh was hastily evacuated, the armed vessels sunk, and a considerable quantity of artillery and stores were abandoned. The regular communication between the different French corps was now lost; and a valuable convoy and two or three detachments were captured. During these operations, the Grand Vizir, with near sixteen thousand men, penetrated into the eastern side of the Delta, and advanced as far as the town of Balbie, on the road to Cairo.

General Hutchinson proceeded up the Nile to Algam; and alarmed, lest the Grand Vizir should be endangered by his forward movement, he wrote to request that he would not risk an action till the British were sufficiently near to give him support. As was foreseen, a strong French force, amounting to four thousand six hundred infantry, and nine hundred cavalry, with twenty-four pieces of cannon, sallied out of Cairo to fall upon the Vizir's army before their junction with the British. The Vizir conceived that, if he retrograded, his undisciplined troops would be so dispirited as to disband; he therefore boldly advanced, and encountered the French at El Hanca. A brisk cannonade ensued, and the advanced corps were engaged for several hours.

The Turks maintained their ground, their cavalry, which was numerous, threatening the flanks of the French; who after fighting deliberately, judged it prudent to retreat to Cairo, baffled in their design, with the loss of three hundred men. This unexpected repulse by an enemy whom before they had always chased from the field with ease, proved how very much the spirit of the French was sunk, and how much the courage of the Turks had been elevated.

General Hutchinson, relieved from his embarrassments, ascended one of the canals of the Nile, in his barge, to Monouf, to congratulate the Grand Vizir on this victory. In his reception, there was a mixture of eastern pomp with grateful respect. He was entertained with a display of horsemanship, and of throwing the dgiredde, a species of mock-fighting in which the Mamelukes excel. They gallop, wheel round, and rein in their Arabian chargers with graceful ease and martial skill.

In the conferences which were held, it was decided that the combined armies should march to besiege Cairo, as soon as the cannon, provisions, and stores could be brought forward. Multitudes of Arabs now crowded to the Vizir's camp; and Osman Bey, with twelve hundred Mamelukes finely equipped, also joined. What a change success had produced! When the handful of British first assailed the conquerors of Egypt, not a sword was raised to help, not a voice was heard to cheer them!—But now Turks, Arabs, Syrians, Copts, and Mamelukes, all vied with friendly aid to expel the French.

With these irregular and uncontrollable allies, and with provisions, stores, and a battering train for the siege, a rapid advance could not be made. Yet little resistance occurred on the march from the enemy, who were concentrating their forces, and strengthening the fortifications of Cairo, with the determination, as was conceived, of retrieving their affairs by a desperate defence.

By General Hutchinson's correspondence, Moore was informed of every passing event. His impatience at the slow healing of his wound augmented as the army advanced; and on its approaching the enemy's stronghold, became irresistible. Though the wound was still open, in defiance of the surgeon's advice, he embarked in a dgerm on the Canopic branch of the Nile; he was towed up the stream and reached the camp before Cairo on the 29th of June. To his surprise, the French General, who had thirteen thousand effective soldiers in the place, was then capitulating without having fired a shot.

In twelve days the French troops went out submissively to Giza, when two British regiments marched into the citadel, and the Turks took possession of the city.

After examining the entrenchments, and seeing the numbers and condition of the French army, General Moore considered the

conduct of their General very disgraceful.
A siege protracted for only two or three
weeks would have greatly reduced the British, who were wasting away with dysentery,
the plague, and, what was worse than both,
ophthalmia : great multitudes were struck
blind by this melancholy malady.

Generals Hutchinson and Craddock both
fell sick, and Moore succeeded to the command, who guarded the French to the sea-
coast to dismiss them from Egypt.

This was a military procession of a most
singular kind. The French who had capitulated were more than twice as numerous
as the British ; but these were supported by
the horde of Turks. As the French retained
their arms, and field-artillery, Moore's prudence led him to take every precaution
against a breach of faith, and a surprise. No
intercourse was permitted between the soldiers of the different nations ; and his troops
were kept night and day ready for action.
The Turks marched first ; the British in the
second line, interposing between the Turks

and the French, who followed next. The British rear-guard always kept sight of the French advanced corps; and the Mameluke cavalry moved last in the rear of the French. The march being conducted with the utmost regularity, no disturbance arose. One day General Moore, having occasion to meet, on business, the French commander, Belliard, asked if he had any objection to his seeing the column pass. An evasive answer was returned, which showed unwillingness.— Moore, from delicacy acquiesced; yet recollected that French Generals are not averse to exhibit their troops when triumphant. Subsequently a change in the order of march enabled him to see their whole line pass by.

The soldiers were fine stout men, and in good spirits at the prospect of returning home. The whole reached the neighbourhood of Rosetta on the 29th of July, and in ten days the embarkation of the French commenced. A few weeks before this, a reinforcement of above eighteen hundred men arrived from England, and General Hutchinson prepared to besiege Alexandria, the only spot in Egypt still held by the French. The fortifications were strong, and the garrison numerous; yet this was an easy enterprise, when compared to those which had been achieved.

The reserve was stationed on the right of the lines, where it had formerly fought. General Craddock superintended the brigades on the left. Five thousand men, under General Coote, were sent round in boats, to invade the west side of the town, who cut off all communication with the country. The French advanced posts were driven in, their sallies repelled, the approaches were begun, and batteries erected against both the eastern and western fronts: the latter being the weakest, the principal attack was made there.

Nothing very memorable occurred in this siege, for as Menou despaired of relief, instead of holding out to the last, he capitulated early; and obtained favourable terms; for it was granted that the French, with all their private property, should be conveyed back to France.

Such was the mortifying conclusion of Bonaparte's conquest of Egypt. And as several ancient sarcophagi and obelisks, the famed triple-inscribed granite stone of Rosetta, a number of statues, Oriental manuscripts, and other Coptic antiquities, were wrested from the plunderers, and embarked for the British Museum, these are long-enduring memorials of this glorious expedition.

On visiting Alexandria, Moore found that the works for the defence of the place, which had been executed since the landing of the British, were prodigious, and what no other but French troops could have effected. He was also struck with the superiority of the French engineers. There now arrived a corps of six thousand Indian troops, under Sir David Baird, which had sailed up the Red Sea. They had encountered storms and contrary winds in their passage to Suez, and had also endured much distress in crossing the deserts; and only reached Alexandria, when the French were embarking to quit the country. Useful co-operation from such a distance is imaginary.

Letters now arrived to General Moore from his family, intimating that his father was declining in health, and earnestly wished for his return. This was conceded to by General Hutchinson without hesitation. Indeed the Duke of York, on learning that Moore had been wounded, wrote to him most kindly, and requested that he would come home, where an arrangement was made for him. This letter he kept back from his Commander until the campaign was finished. He had a prosperous voyage to England, where he arrived, soon after peace had been concluded between Great Britain and France.

END OF VOLUME I.

SD - #0043 - 220221 - C0 - 229/152/18 - PB - 9780282439316